JOCASTA'S CRIME

JOCASTA'S CRIME
AN ANTHROPOLOGICAL STUDY

BY
LORD RAGLAN

NEW YORK
Howard Fertig
1991

First Published in 1991 by Howard Fertig, Inc.
80 East 11th Street, New York, N.Y. 10003
All rights reserved.

Library of Congress Cataloging-in-Publication Data
Raglan, FitzRoy Richard Somerset, Baron, 1885–
  Jocasta's crime : an anthropological study / by Lord Raglan.
    p. cm.
  Reprint. Originally published: London : Methuen, 1933.
  Includes bibliographical references and index.
  ISBN 0-86527-401-0
  1. Incest. 2. Marriage—History. 3. Endogamy and exogamy. 4. Society, Primitive. I. Title.
GN480.25.R34 1991
306.877—dc20   90-40113
                                                    CIP

Reproduced from an original copy
in the Duke University Library

Printed in the United States of America

JOCASTA'S CRIME
AN ANTHROPOLOGICAL STUDY

BY
LORD RAGLAN

METHUEN & CO. LTD.
36 ESSEX STREET W.C.
LONDON

Facsimile of the title page of the original edition.

First Published in 1933

PRINTED IN GREAT BRITAIN

TO
WARREN R. DAWSON

PREFACE

IN the winter of 1929 I happened to read three of the works which will be quoted in the body of this book, and I was struck by the importance which the writers attached to the incest taboo, and the very different origins which they confidently assigned to it. I consulted the works of other writers, and compiled a dozen theories of incest origin, all of them different. Not only did these theories seem to me inadequate and fallacious in themselves, but in no single case did the writer make any attempt to define the term 'incest', or to set out the facts which he professed to explain. In addition, many of the writers, though persons whom one would expect to have a considerable acquaintance with anthropological literature, seemed quite unaware that any theory of incest origin, other than their own, had ever been put forward.

I embodied my criticisms of these theories, together with some suggestions for the solution of the problem, in a paper which was published in 1931 in the Journal of the Royal Anthropological Institute under the title of *Incest and Exogamy*. On its appearance Mr. Warren R. Dawson suggested to me that a book summarizing all the facts and theories relating to the subject would be a useful contribution to anthropological literature. With this idea in mind I embarked upon a long course of reading, during which the conclusion was forced upon me that the theories which I had previously formed, though well enough up to a point, were inadequate to account for the variety and complexity of the phenomena which had to be explained, and my researches took a direction quite different from that which I anticipated when I began.

That the results are incomplete I am only too well aware. There is no bibliography of the subject, and the book has been written in the depths of the country, far from a reference library. My ignorance of German has prevented me from going through the vast amount of material in that language which has not been translated. Finally, in my desire to keep the book within due limits I may sometimes have left out facts that for completeness' sake should have been included.

I should wish to express my gratitude in the first place to the late Mr. A. H. Huth, whose *The Marriage of Near Kin*, though published in 1875, when comparatively little information on the subject was available, seems to me the model of what a scientific monograph should be. Sir James Frazer's works are indispensable, and have been largely used ; and the same may be said of Mr. Briffault's *The Mothers*, in which a vast amount of information is admirably set out.

I have received much help from Mr. Warren R. Dawson ; from Mr. A. M. Hocart, whose *Kingship* is in my opinion the most valuable contribution to the study of social anthropology published during the present century ; from Professor C. Daryll Forde, who has been kind enough to read and suggest many amendments to the MS. ; from Professor and Mrs. C. G. Seligman, though I am afraid that they disagree with many of my views ; from Miss R. M. Fleming,

Librarian of the Royal Anthropological Institute; and from my wife, whose interest in the book has rendered the task of writing it much pleasanter than it would otherwise have been.

Cefntilla Court, Usk,
November 1932

CONTENTS

CHAPTER		PAGE
I.	JOCASTA'S CRIME	1
II.	IS INBREEDING HARMFUL?	8
III.	ARE ANIMALS GOOD FATHERS?	17
IV.	HAVE WE INSTINCTS?	21
V.	IS IT NATURAL FOR MAN TO MATE?	29
VI.	ARE MEN NATURALLY JEALOUS?	33
VII.	WAS MARRIAGE BY CAPTURE ONCE GENERAL?	39
VIII.	DO RELIGIOUS BELIEFS ARISE FROM RATIONAL MEASURES?	46
IX.	WAS EARLY MAN A LEGISLATOR?	51
X.	WAS EARLY MAN A SOCIAL REFORMER?	64
XI.	FREUD'S THEORIES	70
XII.	IS THE INCEST TABOO MAGICAL IN ORIGIN?	76
XIII.	OTHER THEORIES	79
XIV.	SUMMARY OF THEORIES	85
XV.	MAGIC AND TABOO	88
XVI.	WHAT IS INCEST?	98
XVII.	WHY IS A MENSTRUOUS WOMAN TABOO?	109
XVIII.	WHY MUST A MAN AVOID HIS MOTHER-IN-LAW?	116

CHAPTER		PAGE
XIX.	HOW DID EXOGAMY ARISE?	122
XX.	THE DIFFUSION OF CULTURE	130
XXI.	WHAT IS A MYTH?	136
XXII.	INCEST IN MYTH AND RITUAL	144
XXIII.	THE CREATION RITE	163
XXIV.	THE HUSBAND AS BROTHER	170
XXV.	WHAT IS A FATHER?	180
XXVI.	OEDIPUS AND JOCASTA	191
	NOTES	197
	BIBLIOGRAPHY	203
	INDEX	209

ABBREVIATIONS USED IN THE FOOTNOTES

GB—*The Golden Bough*, by Sir James Frazer
FOT—*Folklore in the Old Testament*, by Sir James Frazer
Mothers—*The Mothers*, by Robert Briffault
JRAI—Journal of the Royal Anthropological Institute

JOCASTA'S CRIME

CHAPTER I

JOCASTA'S CRIME

' And loudly o'er the bed she wailed where she
' In twofold wedlock, hapless, had brought forth
' Husband from a husband, children from a child.
' We could not know the moment of her death
' Which followed soon '.
SOPHOCLES : *King Oedipus*

THE story of Oedipus is familiar. The son of Laius, king of Thebes, and Jocasta his queen, he is doomed to death at birth on account of an oracular prophecy, but is secretly saved, and reared at Corinth. On reaching manhood he is told by the oracle at Delphi that he will be guilty of parricide and incest, and believing the king of Corinth to be his father, decides not to return there, and sets forth in another direction. On the road he meets a stranger ; they quarrel and fight, and the stranger, who is his real father, Laius, is killed. Ignorant of his victim's identity, Oedipus proceeds to Thebes, where he finds the Sphinx devouring all who cannot answer her riddles. He overcomes her, and in consequence is made king, and married to the queen, who is his own mother, Jocasta. Many years later a plague descends upon Thebes, and the oracle, on being consulted, says that the only way of staying it is to avenge the death of Laius. Inquiries are made, and the facts at length ascertained. Jocasta hangs herself, and

Oedipus, having put out his eyes, goes into voluntary exile.

The story is mythical, and what that means we shall consider later, but one point clearly emerges: Jocasta's action in marrying her son is regarded as a crime that can only be expiated by her death.

Why was it so regarded? If a modern European were asked why it is a crime for a woman to marry her son he would probably answer either that only a thoroughly depraved woman could be guilty of such an immoral and unnatural act, or else that such a union would produce weakly or imbecile children; but there is nothing in the story of Oedipus which gives the slightest countenance to either of these views. Jocasta was a perfectly innocent and virtuous woman, who believed that her only son was dead; her children by Oedipus, far from being weaklings or imbeciles, were among the most famous heroes and heroines of Greek mythology.

The problem is one which has puzzled theologians, philosophers, and scientists from the earliest times. We shall consider it in detail at a later stage, but here we may obtain a clearer idea of its nature by comparing the story of Oedipus with the view of incest taken in Ashanti at the present day. ' Incest has in ' Ashanti ', says Captain Rattray,[1] ' a much wider ' range of meaning than that word implies in our own ' language. It included sexual intercourse with any- ' one of the same blood or clan, however remote the ' connexion, and even cases where it would not be ' possible to trace direct descent. The bearing of a ' common clan name was considered as conclusive

[1] *Ashanti Law*, p. 304.

'evidence pointing to the existence of a common
'female ancestress. Perhaps no other sin was regarded
'with greater horror among the Ashanti. Both
'parties to the offence were killed. Had such an
'act been allowed to pass unpunished, then, in the
'words of my informants, "hunters would have
'" ceased to kill animals in the forest, the crops would
'" have refused to bear fruit, children would have
'" ceased to be born, the spirits of the dead ancestors
'" would have been infuriated, the gods would have
'" been angered, clans would have ceased to exist,
'" and all would have been chaos in the world ".'
Similarly we are told that in North Borneo incest is
regarded with the utmost horror. 'It is the most
'serious crime in the native law, and formerly the
'penalty was almost invariably death. Even now
'any plague, flood, drought, or famine is ascribed
'to some undetected act of incest'.[1] We shall see
later [2] that the French peasants believe, or believed
up till recent times, that the marriage of first cousins
causes failures of the crops and epidemics among the
flocks.

It is clear then that in Ashanti, in Borneo, and in
France, incest, or the marriage of near kin, is not
a matter of eugenics or of private morality; it is a
national catastrophe, the dread consequences of which
can only be averted by the sacrifice of the guilty
parties; and it would appear that the ancient Greeks
held exactly the same view. It is in fact, as we shall
see later, the normal attitude of the ancient and savage
world. We shall presently examine a score of theories,
in none of which is this fact taken into account.

[1] O. Rutter, *Pagans of North Borneo*, p. 141.   [2] p. 83.

Let us follow Captain Rattray[1] one step further. 'An Ashanti, in olden times, would have been executed 'for marrying or having sexual intercourse with his 'mother's sister's child—he would have committed '"incest" by so doing—yet, at the same time, he 'was enjoined to marry his mother's brother's child'. But while in Ashanti descent is reckoned through the female, in Southern India it is reckoned through the male line, and there, while a man may not marry a member of his father's clan, his proper bride is in many cases his sister's daughter.[2] Dr. Westermarck, then, misleads us when he says that ' as a rule the prohibited 'degrees are more numerous among peoples unaffected 'by modern civilization than they are in more advanced 'communities',[3] since the difference is not one of degree but of kind. Our own incest laws work bilaterally, that is to say that the relatives of both parents are treated in exactly the same way. Among the less civilized, on the other hand, the incest laws work unilaterally, that is to say that the whole of one parent's clan, numbering perhaps thousands of individuals, is absolutely barred, while marriage with near relatives on the other parent's side is permitted, and often enjoined. This fact has also been completely disregarded by the theorists. Since, then, they have, inexcusably in the case of the more recent writers, ignored the two most striking facts which assail any student of the incest taboo, it is not surprising that they have failed to find the correct solution of the problem. It is, of course, quite possible that I also have failed, but at any rate I have taken into account

---

[1] Loc. cit. [2] FOT, II, pp. 113-16.
[3] E. Westermarck, *Origin and Development of Moral Ideas*, II, p. 366.

all the relevant facts which I have been able to ascertain. As the end of the book is approached my solution will be gradually unfolded, but perhaps it will be as well to indicate here the nature of the framework upon which it will be laid.

Let us first deal with the question of unilateral kinship. We have seen that in Ashanti it was a capital offence for a man to marry a woman of his mother's clan, however remote the connexion, while he was enjoined to marry his father's sister's daughter; and, on the other hand, that in Southern India a man must not marry a woman of his father's clan, but often marries his own sister's daughter. It seems clear that these laws and customs are not intended to prevent inbreeding, not merely because they obviously do nothing of the kind, but also because, as we shall see presently, the idea of inbreeding is completely absent from the uncivilized mind. Nor have they any connexion with a preference for strange women, since a man's prescribed bride is not merely a kinswoman, but, as a rule, a girl whom he has known all his life. The law of exogamy, that is out-marriage, means that a man or woman must marry outside a group which usually consists of his or her clan-fellows. It is as if two unrelated persons might not marry if they were both called Smith, but that Mr. Smith might marry Miss Brown, even if she were his sister's daughter. Fantastic theories have been based on the belief that savages have to marry outside their own tribe; such a rule is totally unknown.

Incest among savages is simply a breach of the law of exogamy, and since exogamy has no connexion with a preference for non-relatives, the incest taboo, as it exists among savages, has equally no connexion with a preference for non-relatives. This simple fact is sufficient to dispose of most of the theories which have been put forward to account for the origin of the incest taboo, though when we come to examine them we shall find that they all fail on other grounds as well. Most of them are based on the belief that the origin of the incest taboo is either rational or instinctive, but it is clearly irrational to compel a man to marry one first cousin and put him to death if he marries another, while to suppose that Mr. Smith and Miss Smith instinctively avoid each other is absurd.

Some writers have supposed that the taboo had a religious origin, but it is most stringently enforced by savages such as the Australian blacks, who cannot be said to have a religion unless we are prepared to give the word 'religion' two quite different meanings.

Having eliminated reason, instinct, and religion as bases of the incest taboo, what have we left ? The answer is magic. Magic will be dealt with at length in a later chapter, but it may here be briefly defined as a belief that some things are 'lucky' and others 'unlucky'. It is universal among savages, and almost universal among members of more civilized communities. It is quite unconnected with belief in a deity, and is not only far more widespread but in all probability far more ancient than any religious belief.

There are a great many institutions to which we may confidently assign a magical origin, and the belief, found in at least three continents, that incest causes failure of the crops, encourages us to place it among them. We shall later find reason to believe not merely that the incest taboo has a magical origin, but that to commit incest is the most 'unlucky' thing that any one can do.

I shall now proceed to examine in detail the theories to which I have referred, and I shall do this for two reasons : firstly, because some of them are too deeply entrenched to be driven out without a regular assault ; and secondly, because in levelling their works I shall at the same time be preparing the foundations for what I believe to be a more permanent and defensible fortress.

CHAPTER II

IS INBREEDING HARMFUL?

WE have seen that there is no natural horror of
'incest, and that many peoples have practised
'it and do practise it; while, on the other
'hand, we have seen that whatever may be the reasons
'of certain prohibitions which exist, they are certainly
'not due to any conscious or unconscious experience of
'evil results. We have seen that the statistics on which
'so much reliance has been placed, as a proof of the
'harmfulness of consanguineous marriage, are, when
'not absolutely false, miserably misleading and defec-
'tive. And, finally, we have seen that the great argu-
'ment of biologists that crosses must be beneficial or
'there would not be two sexes is by no means proved,
'and the presence of dual sex can be accounted for in
'another way. On the other hand we have seen many
'cases of in-and-in breeding in isolated communities,
'and more especially among domestic animals, in which
'no evil effects have been observed.'

These words occur in the concluding chapter of *The Marriage of Near Kin*, by A. H. Huth, published in 1875. Mr. Huth tells us that ' the Egyptians were accustomed ' to marry their sisters from the earliest times of which ' we have any record ',[1] and that the Persians married not only their sisters, but also their mothers and daughters, apparently with no ill effects. He goes on to give a large number of cases in which consanguineous

---

[1] See also GB, VI, p. 214; Mothers, I, p. 384; Sir W. Ridgeway, *The Origin of Tragedy*, p. 197.

marriage is allowed by law, and points out that the Mosaic law does not forbid the marriage of uncle and niece. He gives numerous examples of inbred communities and inbred families, the members of which are perfectly healthy, such as the Pitcairn Islanders, all descended from the mutineers of the Bounty; the Tengger Hills community of Java, who though closely inbred from time immemorial are the biggest and strongest people on the island; and the Forèatines of the department of Cher, who though all descended from marriages between near kin formed one of the handsomest races in France. Only one Stuart of Glenfinlass had ever married outside the glen, yet all were healthy. He gives many other examples of human and also of animal groups. We shall consider the animals later.

The most commonly alleged ill effects of consanguineous marriage are sterility, idiocy, and deaf-mutism. Huth shows that attempts to prove these effects are completely unreliable, since there are no accurate statistics for consanguineous marriages in any country, and the estimates of the writers whom he quotes differ widely from each other. He also shows how with an uncertain classification and a small number of cases figures can be made to prove anything. The believers in the harmfulness of inbreeding were not content with deaf-mutism and idiocy, but included among its results meningitis, convulsions, croup, whooping-cough, goitre, rickets, and other diseases with which heredity has little or nothing to do.

Huth considered it probable that the belief that consanguineous marriage leads to sterility is due to a misinterpretation of Leviticus xx. 20: 'If a man shall

'lie with his uncle's wife . . . they shall die childless,
'and if a man shall take his brother's wife they shall
'be childless'. A man is no relation to his brother's
wife, and the passage is clearly a curse on adulterers
and not a statement of biological fact.

The conclusions which Mr. Huth reached more than
fifty years ago are identical with those of Mr. Briffault,
who says [1]: 'The belief that inbreeding is injurious
'to the race, and that, in particular, the offspring of
'individuals who are closely related by blood is liable
'to suffer from various afflictions and to be of low
'vitality has been practically universal from time
'immemorial, and has been held by many distinguished
'men of science. It is only since the end of the last
'century that endeavours have been made to inquire
'into the grounds of that belief, and to substantiate it
'by a reference to facts. These attempts have resulted
'in complete failure.'

He goes on to give examples of inbreeding among
animals. Union between brother and sister is the rule
with tigers, buffaloes, red deer, and many species of
antelopes. Horses, cattle, dogs, and monkeys live in
small groups which keep strictly to themselves and
never mate with outsiders. Throughout the animal
world there is a universal reluctance to mate outside
the variety, even where the difference between two
varieties is slight.

Whole countries have been overrun in a short time
by the offspring of a few individuals, or even of a
single pair. All the rabbits in Australia are descended
from a few brought there in 1863. A boar and two
sows brought to New Zealand by Captain Cook had

[1] Mothers, I, p. 204.

IS INBREEDING HARMFUL?

a vast number of descendants. Eleven horses were turned loose in the Argentine in 1535; by the end of the century there were enormous herds. These and many other cases show no sign of ill effects from inbreeding.

Many experiments have been made with domestic animals, but in no case has disease or debility resulted from inbreeding. In some cases there has been a diminution of fertility, but this is to be attributed to close confinement, since this affects all animals, and many wild animals will not breed in captivity at all. In one case rats were paired brother and sister for twenty-two generations; the resulting animals were considerably heavier than and much superior in every way to the stock rats. A prize bull was matched with his daughter, granddaughter and great-granddaughter; the offspring of the latter, a cow, had 93·75 per cent of the blood of the breeding bull. She was matched with a bull which had 62·5 per cent of the blood of the same animal, and the resulting offspring realized the breeder's highest dreams of perfection.

The belief of breeders that occasional crosses are beneficial is due in part to the fact that the fatness of the prize pig is really a pathological condition, and unless these pigs are occasionally crossed with something nearer to the normal, they become so fat that they cease to breed. The English thoroughbred horse was inbred for about two centuries, during which time it continuously improved; since then it has been bred solely to win short races at an early age, and has deteriorated.

Since an occasional cross is beneficial only when stock has been bred injudiciously for some artificial quality, many successful breeders of cattle and dogs never cross their stock. In Central Europe stock-breeding was for long a failure owing to the authority of a certain Professor Settegast, who inveighed fiercely against the supposed evils of inbreeding; it was not until the Germans became convinced that his theories were unsound that they were able to breed scientifically and to become independent of imported stock.

There is not, in the records of inbreeding from domestic animals, a single fact which suggests, much less proves, that the closest inbreeding is in itself productive of evil effects.

In the human race the evidence of facts is, if anything, even more definite than among animals. Most savages are exogamous, that is to say, they marry outside the clan or other group; this means, in very many cases, that a man marries the daughter either of his mother's brother or his father's sister. Some are endogamous, that is to say they marry within the group; this usually means that a man marries his father's brother's daughter. Marriage with a first cousin, in one form or the other, has been practised by many races from time immemorial without the slightest ill effect. Among the Arabs a man almost invariably marries his first cousin, yet Doughty says that 'not-' withstanding the affinity in all their wedlock, there ' was none deformed or lunatic among those robust ' hill Beduins'. Speaking of the same people Burton says: 'Here no evil results are anticipated from the ' union of first cousins, and the experience of ages and ' of a mighty nation may be trusted.' A census of Fiji showed that marriage between first cousins was associated with a higher birth-rate and a markedly

IS INBREEDING HARMFUL?

greater vitality in the offspring than union between non-relatives.[1]

Much of the evidence which Mr. Briffault adduces merely confirms the conclusions of Huth; but on one point he goes beyond him—one of the commonest beliefs concerning the marriage of near kin is that it causes deaf-mutism in the offspring; Mr. Briffault adduces much evidence to suggest that there is no such thing as hereditary deaf-mutism, but that deaf-mutism is the result of post-natal infection or insanitary conditions in early childhood. He concludes that the European belief that the children of consanguineous marriages are unhealthy is a superstition akin to the belief of the Aleuts that the offspring of an incestuous union would have tusks like a walrus; of the people of Celebes that such unions produce failure of the crops; of the Galelarese that they cause earthquakes and volcanic eruptions, and of the people of Mindanao that they cause floods.[2]

Though some eminent scientists still believe in the evil effects of inbreeding others do not. Thus Sir Arthur Thomson tells us [3] that ' close endogamy does ' not seem in itself to induce degeneracy unless there ' are marked hereditary taints and defects in the ' inbreeding stock '. It does not of course require endogamy to induce degeneracy in the offspring of individuals with marked hereditary taints and defects. Professor F. A. E. Crew, the distinguished biologist, says [4] ' It is now known that outcrossing, which in- ' volves the mating of two dissimilar types, does not

---

[1] The foregoing is abridged from *The Mothers*, I, pp. 204–18.
[2] Op. cit., pp. 238–9.   [3] *An Outline of Modern Knowledge*, p. 248.
[4] Ibid., p. 261.

'invariably yield hybrid vigour, and also that inbreeding is not always harmful, but that, in fact, it can be definitely advantageous, leading to the establishment of a uniform and true-breeding stock.' He goes on to explain how the inbreeding of healthy stocks leads to improvement and that of unhealthy stocks to extinction, while outcrossing tends to the production of individuals who are sound in some respects and unsound in others. It would seem, in short, that outcrossing makes for quantity and inbreeding for quality. Among our early ancestors it was probably quality that counted.

There is one other point: it is generally held that the whole human race is descended from a single group, and if this is so, and unless the effects of climate on physique are much greater than scientists believe, it must have taken long periods of close inbreeding to produce the very varied types of humanity which now inhabit the earth.

It may be objected that though there are in fact no ill effects from inbreeding, yet since many people now believe that inbreeding causes weakly offspring, early man may well have thought the same. Apart from the fact that in Europe the belief that inbreeding causes weakly offspring does not appear to be more than three hundred years old [1] and that among savages it is floods and famines, rather than weakly offspring, which are believed to be caused by breaches of the incest taboo, it is now well established that over a considerable part of the savage world conception is believed to have nothing to do with the father, who is the father merely because he is the mother's husband. This belief, or rather this ignorance, is reported from

[1] See below, p. 83.

IS INBREEDING HARMFUL?

many parts of Australia, and from New Guinea, New Caledonia, the Trobriand Islands, and Central Borneo.[1] In these areas women, according as they wish or do not wish for children, perform or refrain from certain actions, such as walking near burial-places, bathing in the sea, and eating particular foods. Similar beliefs were held in many parts of the world. Rachel conceived Joseph by eating mandrakes.[2] Zoroaster was conceived through his mother's eating milk mixed with 'homa', and the Irish hero Cuchulain through his mother's eating a worm. Pliny, Virgil, and St. Augustine believed that mares could be fertilized by the wind,[3] and a modern Moorish proverb expresses the same belief with regard to baboons.

There are no stronger upholders of the incest taboo than those very Australian tribes who believe that the child has no physical connexion with the father; and it is quite clear that people who believed that women were fertilized not by living men but by ancestral spirits and other agencies could not possibly believe in the evil effects of inbreeding. The latter belief is an effect and not the cause of the taboo. We can dismiss the opinion of anthropologists of the last century, such as L. H. Morgan and Sir E. B. Tylor, that exogamy was adopted to avoid the observed ill effects of inbreeding, since not only are there no ill effects, but our early ancestors could have had no conception of inbreeding.

Dr. Westermarck's theory is at the first glance more plausible; he supposes[4] that 'consanguineous

---

[1] Prof. B. Malinowski in *Man*, 1932, 44, and note p. 197.
[2] FOT, II, p. 373. [3] Mothers, II, pp. 450-5.
[4] E. Westermarck, *History of Human Marriage*, 1st ed., p. 546. In his later editions he replaces the word 'instinct' by the word 'sentiment', which is meaningless unless defined.

'marriages, in some way or other, are more or less detri-
'mental to the species. Through natural selection an
'instinct must have been developed, powerful enough,
'as a rule, to prevent injurious unions. . . . This
'instinct displays itself simply as an aversion on the
'part of individuals to intercourse with those with
'whom they have lived, but as these are for the most
'part blood relations, the result is the survival of the
'fittest'.

We shall discuss instinct presently; here I will merely point out that Dr. Westermarck assumes, in the face of all the evidence, that inbreeding is harmful, and that he confuses with outbreeding the system of exogamy, which may permit, as in fact in parts of New Guinea and the Solomon Islands it does permit,[1] fathers to marry their own daughters, since under the matrilineal system the latter belong to their mothers' clan. Finally, by postulating an instinctive aversion to intercourse between those who have lived together, he invites us to regard the cohabitation of husband and wife as unnatural.

In making the suggestion, already adumbrated by Dr. Robertson Smith,[2] that the origin of the incest taboo is to be sought in nearness of residence rather than in nearness of blood, he has, however, provided us with a valuable clue, and one that will be followed up in Chapter XIX.

---

[1] *Mothers*, I, p. 257.
[2] *Kinship and Marriage Among the Semites*, p. 201.

CHAPTER III

ARE ANIMALS GOOD FATHERS?

THERE is a widespread belief that the behaviour of animals in their domestic relationships—their courtings, their matings, and their parenthood—is very similar to our own, but this is an illusion which a very slight acquaintance with life on the farm should suffice to dispel. The bull moping because the cow of his choice has spurned his advances; the ram seeking out the choicest pastures and leading the ewe thither; the boar taking the little pigs for a walk while their mother enjoys a needed rest—these may flourish in children's books, but they bear not the slightest resemblance to anything that happens in real life. What really happens is that during the pairing season any male is ready to mate with any female, and vice versa; when two males approach the same female they fight until one kills or drives off the other, after which the victor pairs with the female, who has neither the opportunity nor the desire to exercise any choice. In most cases the animals separate after union, in some cases they remain together for a few weeks or months, but the male does nothing to help the female, who is in no need of assistance, and when the little ones are born she takes good care to hide them from their father, who is apt to kill and eat them, as indeed is the mother herself, though her tendency to do so ceases after the first day or two. In the case of some animals, such as the ruminants, the young are born so fully developed that they stand little chance of being eaten, but there is no evidence in their case, or in that of any other animal, that the father takes the smallest part in feeding, protecting, or training his offspring.

It may well be asked what all this has to do with the incest taboo; the answer is that Professor Malinowski has put forward a theory of incest origin based on the supposition that among certain animals which he vaguely describes sometimes as ' mammals ' and sometimes as ' higher mammals ' the male plays the part of husband and father in the most exemplary manner. When approaching a female he restrains his instincts until other males appear on the scene, ' for there must ' be opportunities for comparison and for choice with ' either sex '. Mating accomplished, the male ' guards, ' assists, protects, and nourishes ' the ' helpless ' female in her pregnancy, and when the offspring are born, joins with the female in providing ' care and training ' until they become independent.[1]

Professor Malinowski's language is somewhat obscure; he seems to suppose that such behaviour is characteristic of all mammals, but even among higher mammals we find nothing to support his suppositions. The felidae are usually included among the higher mammals, but wild lions, tigers, and leopards have been known to kill and eat their mates, while in captivity jaguars have done the same thing, and so have many other kinds of mammal, including bears, wolves, and mice.[2] Among most carnivora male and female only live together for a short time during the mating season, and in many species there is no

---

[1] B. Malinowski, *Sex and Repression in Savage Society*, p. 197.
[2] *Mothers*, I, pp. 118 seq.

cohabitation at all; two adult bears have never been found in one den. In none of these species does the male take any part in rearing the young, and in most cases the female hides herself and her young from him; even when he continues to associate with her, he feeds neither her nor the young.

As regards the apes and monkeys the evidence is less conclusive, but it appears that while these animals are not in the habit of devouring their mates and offspring, in other respects their behaviour differs little from that of the carnivora; they go about in troops of both sexes, in which the males tend to keep apart from the females and young, whom they neither guard nor feed.

Many of these facts are easily ascertainable; some indeed are obvious to any one who has observed, even superficially, the habits of the domestic cat. How is it, then, that so many people fail to recognize them? The answer probably is that most people have so little imagination that they suppose that everything to which they are accustomed is 'natural', and is therefore common not only to the whole human race, but to the whole animal world as well. Most people, again, both civilized and savage, are brought up on stories, of the type of Aesop's Fables, in which animals are represented as acting, thinking, and even talking, exactly like human beings; and in most cases the impressions thus acquired are not corrected by education. Further, in this particular case, a false analogy is drawn from the mating arrangements of the nest-building birds, which are in some respects comparable to monogamous human marriage.

Having been led astray, either by these causes or by

others, into crediting the mammals with all these instinctive virtues, Professor Malinowski goes on to suppose that man, when he became man, lost both his instincts and his virtues, and proceeded to neglect and maltreat his wife and children most disgracefully. But though his conduct was low, his ideals were high ; the conservative tendency so distressingly prevalent among his degenerate descendants was completely absent from his political complex ; the idea of progress was ever present in his mind, and when he found progress slow in coming, he took counsel with his fellows and imposed upon himself the incest and other taboos, thereby raising himself to the level of social morality already reached instinctively by the brutes.

The idea of progress is of course quite a recent one, even in Western Europe ; the fallacy of supposing that early man was a sociologist and a legislator will be dealt with later ; the more serious fallacy that people can be made virtuous by Act of Parliament is outside the scope of this book. The recent researches of Yerkes,[1] and Zuckerman,[2] enable us to state with some confidence that the study of animal behaviour is unlikely to throw the smallest light upon the origin of human customs and institutions.

---

[1] R. M. and A. W. Yerkes, *The Great Apes*.
[2] S. Zuckerman, *The Social Life of Monkeys and Apes*.

CHAPTER IV

HAVE WE INSTINCTS?

THE answer to this question depends of course on what we understand by the word 'instinct'; a satisfactory definition of the word is not easy to find, and few of those who use the word make any attempt to define it. We are all agreed that animals have instincts, and unless we are to have two definitions of the word, we must limit it, in its application to man, to activities which man has, or can be supposed to have, in common with the lower animals. When, therefore, we find Dr. Havelock Ellis [1] writing of 'Quetelet, who instinctively scented unreclaimed 'fields of statistical investigation', we must, unless we assume that Dr. Ellis used the word inadvertently—such carelessness is unfortunately only too common among scientific writers—hasten to dissociate ourselves with any definition of instinct which could possibly include the possession of such a faculty.

Professor McDougall, oblivious of the fact that human beings act differently while animals of the same species always act in the same manner, attributes most human activities to instinct. He supposes, for example, that man builds houses because he has an 'instinct of construction' [2] an instinct which Sir Edwin Lutyens apparently shares with the bees, but not with the natives of Central Australia and Tierra del Fuego, who live completely houseless.

While on the one hand we should not use the word

---

[1] *Studies*, I, p. 137.   [2] W. McDougall, *Social Psychology*, p. 88.

for purely human faculties, we must on the other hand beware of applying it to actions which are purely reflex, that is to say, where a given stimulus invariably produces a given response without any opportunity for volition on the part of the respondent. Many writers have described the action of a newly-born babe in sucking as instinctive, but Professor Hobhouse, whose views on instinct we shall discuss in a moment, describes it [1] as 'purely reflex'; it appears to be well established that babies and young animals will suck anything that finds its way into their mouths, and have to be taught the proper place to suck.

As an example of instinctive activity let us take the mating of wood-pigeons; they can choose their mate, but it must be another wood-pigeon, and not a stock dove or rock-dove, birds of very similar appearance; they can choose the tree for their nest, but the nest must be in a tree, and made in a particular way with particular materials; so with the hatching of the eggs and the feeding of the young birds a certain course must be followed, but not in a hard and fast manner.

There are two facts to be noted: first that the birds know how to build a nest and hatch eggs without having seen it done; second that the wood-pigeons' ancestors built on the ground or on rocks, and though they have built in trees for a very long time, they have not yet acquired the art of building a really suitable nest, with the result that a large proportion of the eggs and young birds fall from the nest and perish. Bees again have just sufficient instinctive ability to

---

[1] L. T. Hobhouse, *Mind in Evolution*, p. 34.

enable them to survive; had they the slightest real intelligence, the whole subarctic world would be alive with them.

I will then define instinct as that which impels an animal, without the necessity for instruction or imitation, to follow a certain course of life—a course which, though not necessarily the best adapted to its needs, often, but by no means invariably, enables it to maintain itself and reproduce its kind.

Another fact to be noted about instinct is that it is a succession of stimuli, and cannot therefore be prohibitive in its action. A chicken is not prohibited from entering the water; it does not do so because it lacks the necessary stimulus. It has been suggested to me that the avoidance of bad smells is instinctive, but a little reflection will show that this is a fallacy; the nastiest smells are harmless, and one of the nastiest smells to us, that of decaying flesh, is one of the pleasantest to carnivorous animals and to savage man, for it brings the promise of a full stomach with little effort. We perhaps owe the survival of our sense of smell to the fact that with early man the fittest to survive were those who could smell carrion the farthest.

Those who postulate an instinctive origin for the incest taboo should suggest an explanation of how an instinct arose in man, differing both in kind and in character from anything which exists among animals, and saying 'thou shalt not' so forcibly that he was compelled to exchange the near, safe, and familiar for the remote, dangerous, and strange. This, so far as I can learn, they have completely failed to do, nor, in postulating such a complex instinct, have they attempted to account for the fact that the simplest, most universal, and what would seem the most necessary instinct in the world, that which teaches the mother how to look after her young, is completely non-existent in the human female. Many, if not most, of the ills from which we suffer are due to improper feeding or other improper treatment in early childhood. Is it instinct which induces the human mother, both savage and civilized, to fill her baby's stomach with meat; to bind it so tightly that it cannot move; to deny it light and air? The fact is that instinct has been completely replaced by a mass of foolish customs and superstitions, against which science is struggling, so far with very limited success. Dr. Westermarck thought, as we saw in Chapter II, that an instinct against inbreeding arose because it is 'somehow or other more 'or less detrimental', but there is no 'somehow or 'other' and no 'more or less' about the improper treatment of infants; it militates more than any other single cause against the health and efficiency of the human race; yet not only has no instinct arisen to prevent it, but the instinct which once existed has ceased to exist.

Let us now turn to Professor L. T. Hobhouse, who is one of the chief exponents of the view that the horror of incest is instinctive; it will be necessary to quote him [1] at some length:

'Notwithstanding the great variation in the forms 'which it takes, the exogamic impulse seems to per-'form certain functions which are fairly constant. 'Thus (1) it checks in-and-in breeding, barring inter-'marriage with near kin. . . . What, precisely, are 'the physical disadvantages of in-and-in breeding or

[1] *Morals in Evolution*, p. 145.

'the advantages of crossing is, however, harder to say
'than is popularly supposed, and it is probable that
'this biological side of the matter is the least important
'of the functions served by exogamy. But (2) . . . it
'has the important sociological function of binding
'distinct groups together. (3) A third function of
'more importance in the civilized world is of a dis-
'tinctly ethical character. For us the prohibition of
'incest is the only form of exogamy which persists,
'and incest is a crime which infects us with a horror,
'of the kind we call instinctive, and which is certainly
'not weaker in civilized than in barbarous humanity.
'What is the meaning of this horror? It is too real
'and deeply rooted to be explained as a survival. It is
'not based on tradition and convention, for it is not
'felt in relation to many crimes which the law forbids.
'Thus among people who accept the law of the Roman
'Church, the marriage of cousins is forbidden, but
'frequently occurs. In our own country men may
'approve or condemn marriage with a deceased wife's
'sister, but any one who would put it on a par with
'incest with a blood-sister would be a very abnormally
'constituted person. Is the horror, then, of incest
'instinctive? The usual objections to this view are
'based on a misunderstanding of instinct. It is said
'that the horror is not universal, and that the objects
'to which it is directed differ widely in different
'peoples. But many instincts in the animal kingdom
'fail in universality and are modifiable in their applica-
'tion. And as we have seen, what is instinctive or
'hereditary in human nature becomes more and more
'a feature of character, a tendency of disposition to
'feel or act which obtains its actual direction from

'experience, and especially from education and social
'tradition. So far as such tendencies are to be ex-
'plained, it must be by showing the function which
'they serve'.

Having failed to find a rational explanation which satisfied him, Professor Hobhouse fell back upon instinct, and realizing that animal instinct, however modifiable, could not possibly obtain its direction from tradition, he invented for humanity a type of instinct totally unknown in the animal world; at least he called it instinct, but in fact it is not instinct at all, but our old friend the innate idea, which though long ago scotched by Locke, was not killed, and here reappears in disguise.

But the professor is still not quite satisfied. The tendency to learn from experience and tradition is instinctive, but in case it is not instinctive, we can explain it by its function; we must explain the horror of incest by its functions of checking inbreeding and binding distinct groups, and by a third function 'of 'a distinctively ethical character'. As regards the first two, it cannot be repeated too often that exogamy does not prevent inbreeding; that it does not bind together distinct groups; and that there is not the slightest evidence that it ever did so. As regards the third function, it is difficult to see how an instinct can be ethical, or how it can be a function of the horror of incest to inculcate a horror of incest. When he speaks of Christian marriages, the professor overlooks the very obvious fact that while marriage with a blood-sister is both a mortal sin and a serious crime, marriage with a cousin or sister-in-law is neither. It is, as we saw in Chapter I, quite untrue to say that the horror of incest is 'certainly not weaker in civilized than in 'barbarous humanity'.

That a custom can be explained by its functions is a complete fallacy. The functions of a custom, in so far as they exist objectively, and not merely in the mind of the observer, are the effects which the custom has on the members of the community in which it is observed, and the effect of a custom obviously cannot be its cause. Let us take the custom of burning to death persons holding unfashionable views on religion; to the bigot its function is to extirpate heresy; to the populace it serves as an awful warning against the abominable practice of thinking for oneself; to the reformer its function is, by arousing the indignation of the more civilized, to hasten on the reformation; while its function to the fuel contractor is to provide him with a livelihood. None of these functions explains the custom, not even the first; there are limits to the cruelty even of religious bigots, and they would probably have been content to see their victims more humanely slaughtered. The custom of burning people alive is far older than religious bigotry, and probably had its origin in an early fertility rite, in which the ashes of a human victim were scattered over the fields as a kind of magical manure.[1] Similarly there is no doubt that the incest taboo is far older than any function which it performs, or can be supposed to perform, in any existing society.

In chasing the red herring of function, which we may suspect that Professor Hobhouse deliberately drew across our path, we have gone far from instinct; let us return to the trail by noting that while the

[1] M. A. Murray, *The Witch-cult in Western Europe*, pp. 159 seq.

professor more than once couples the horror of incest with the horror of witchcraft, he does not venture to suggest that the latter is instinctive.

It is remarkable that the theory here criticized seems so satisfactory to the distinguished American anthropologist, Professor Lowie, that he accepts it without hesitation or comment.[1]

---

[1] R. H. Lowie, *Primitive Society*, p. 14.

CHAPTER V

IS IT NATURAL FOR MAN TO MATE?

In his classic work *Studies in the Psychology of Sex* Dr. Havelock Ellis expresses the opinion that the avoidance of incest, while not instinctive, is 'natural', and before discussing his reasons for so thinking, let us first consider the word 'natural'. The general tendency of mankind is to regard everything to which they are accustomed as natural; Europeans think it natural to wear clothes, while the natives of Central Africa more properly think it natural to go stark naked. The word is often, though clearly not by Dr. Ellis, used as a synonym for 'instinctive'. It is also used to express physical inevitability; breathing is natural and so is death; death from decapitation is not natural death, though it would be unnatural to live without a head. It is commonly used in opposition to 'artificial', yet since there is little agreement as to which is which, this contrast is not very helpful. One further use may be mentioned; an idiot or half-wit is termed a 'natural', and with some justification, since such persons are to a much smaller extent than normal people subject to the restraints imposed by society. To this point we shall return; meanwhile we can safely say that it is impossible to define scientifically a word which is used colloquially in so many different senses, and the word is therefore used sparingly by careful writers.

In Dr. Ellis's view [1] incest avoidance is natural

[1] Op. cit., IV, p. 204.

because, in the case of brothers and sisters, it ' is due
' to the absence of the conditions which tend to produce
' sexual tumescence, and the play of those sensory
' allurements which lead to sexual selection '. In
that case it would be unnecessary to forbid it, since
except in the case of relatives who were separated in
infancy, and did not meet till they were grown up, it
could not possibly occur. But, as almost any assize
calendar will show, its occurrence in this country is by
no means rare. It is frequent between brothers and
sisters, and between widowers and their daughters;
it is most frequent among those imbeciles or ' naturals '
among whom, according to Dr. Ellis's theory, impossibility should be raised to its highest power.[1]

It seems to me that in the whole of this argument
Dr. Ellis has put the cart before the horse. It is not
the case that sensory allurements lead to sexual selection, but rather that artificially restricted sexual
selection leads to the necessity for sensory allurements.
These allurements, or at any rate many of them, such
as scent, cosmetics, frills, and partial exposure, are
the artificial products of culture, and the necessary
consequences of compulsory chastity. Prohibitions
lead to inhibitions, and these inhibitions must be overcome before sexuality can be aroused. A man is not,
as Dr. Ellis supposes, attracted to a woman because she
is different from his sister; on the contrary, the fact
is that if a woman wishes to attract a man she must
first overcome his inhibitions by differentiating herself
from the class of prohibited women, which normally

[1] ' Too often, as at this Assize, girls become pregnant by their
own fathers . . . and there is also at the present Assize a horrible
case where a mentally defective girl was pregnant by her own brother.'
Mr. Justice McCardie at Leeds, December 11th, 1931.

includes not only his sisters, but all his female relatives and all married women, and frequently also those differing from him in race, religion, and social status. These inhibitions, though differing in strength, are of the same character. In the words of two American writers :

'What happens is that the powerful stress of sex-passion is actually neutralized by the mores, for the very existence of even sex-attraction is deemed shameful. This case of the suppression of what is perhaps the strongest of human passions by convention forms one of the best illustrations of the disciplinary control exercised by the mores.'[1]

Dr. Ellis goes on to state that 'brothers and sisters in relation to each other have already reached that state to which old married couples gradually approximate'. This sentence seems to me to contain three fallacies which could be shown to be such from his own works—that old married couples cannot retain an active sexual attraction for each other ; that a state of sexual hunger is psychologically equivalent to a state of sexual satiation ; and that brothers and sisters never take a sexual interest in each other.

Every day we see among ourselves marriages taking place between neighbours who have known each other from the cradle, and between people who have been associated intimately but platonically for years. Dr. Ellis's theory is still less applicable to savages, since among them sensory allurements are often absent, and sexual tumescence is in many cases induced not by individual members of the opposite sex, but by dances and feasts in which numbers of both sexes take part.

[1] Sumner and Keller, *The Science of Society*, p. 1581.

Further, it seems never to have occurred to Dr. Ellis, or to any one holding similar views, that before you can show that it is natural to avoid mating with certain persons, you must first show that mating is itself natural, that is to say, that every one has an innate tendency to pair off with a member of the opposite sex. This question could be discussed at length, but I will content myself with expressing my belief that a man who had never seen or heard of women would never miss them, and that if one were suddenly presented to him he would at first regard her not as supplying a long-felt want, but as a freak of nature.

That it is all a question, not of nature, but of custom, was realized by Montaigne, with his usual good sense :
' This is the receipt by which Plato undertaketh to
' banish the unnatural and preposterous loves of his time,
' and which he esteemeth Soveraigne and principall ;
' To wit, that publike opinion may condemn them ;
' that Poets, and all men else may tell horrible tales of
' them. A receit by meanes whereof the fairest
' daughters winne no more the love of their fathers,
' nor brethren most excellent in beautie the love of
' their sisters. The very fables of Thyestes, of Oedipus,
' and of Macareus, having with the pleasures of their
' songs infused this profitable opinion in the tender
' conceit of children.' [1]

---

[1] Montaigne's *Essays*, Bk. I, Chap. XXII, ' Of Custom '.

CHAPTER VI

ARE MEN NATURALLY JEALOUS?

THE theory of incest origin propounded by the late J. J. Atkinson in his *Primal Law* is based on the assumption that we are descended from gorillas, or from animals with the habits of gorillas. Man is no doubt descended from an ape-like animal, but there is no evidence that that animal was a gorilla, or behaved as such. Atkinson's theory—it is no more—of the habits of gorillas is that among them a group consists of an old male with his wives and children; as his daughters reach maturity he takes them as wives; as his sons reach maturity he gives them a good hiding and turns them out of the group. They then wander about, either alone or with other young males, until by force or cunning, they can obtain a female and set up for themselves. Forty years ago, when Atkinson wrote, little was known for certain about the habits of gorillas; not much more is known now, and what is known leaves it at least doubtful whether they really behave in this way.[1]

Primitive man, according to Atkinson, went on like that until one day, by a happy combination of fortuitous circumstances, a mother succeeded in persuading the old man to let her youngest son remain in the group after he had reached puberty; 'pure 'maternal love triumphed over the demons of lust 'and jealousy',[2] but on one condition; the youth

---

[1] R. M. and A. W. Yerkes, *The Great Apes*, pp. 430 seq.
[2] Op. cit., p. 231.

had to promise not to look upon any of the females in the group with the eye of desire. This promise he readily gave and faithfully kept, and thus instituted the Primal Law, from which followed all social institutions, and especially ' the superlative fact . . . that ' certain females are now to become sacred to certain ' males '.[1]

We might continue to pursue Atkinson's ingenious hypotheses, by which he traces all the rules of incest and avoidance found anywhere in the world to this Primal Law, and the equally ingenious riders of Drs. Hose and McDougall,[2] if we had not already as many fallacies as can conveniently be dealt with in one chapter.

First as regards the primal family ; whatever may be the case with the gorilla, which lives in tropical Africa, it seems evident that if man evolved from an ape-like animal he could only have done so under conditions which placed the highest possible premium on intelligence and activity, and that these qualities could only display themselves in relation to the food supply. It is inconceivable that man could have risen from the animals, or developed anything but a bad temper, merely by conforming to the behaviour of the bull or the stallion, but easy to suppose that he did so by managing to live where his fellows starved. In any hunting community the women, who must carry or remain near the young children, cannot move very far or very fast, and under harsh conditions the men must provide the bulk of the food supply. In such conditions as I have supposed there must have been an optimum number of persons to each group, and this,

[1] p. 236. [2] *Pagan Tribes of Borneo*, Vol. II, pp. 197–8.

as far as the men were concerned, would be such as to provide an adequate number for hunting, while allowing for casualties. In the one-man group, the one man has only to stub his toe, and the group disintegrates or starves.

Now to the law; in his *Primal Law* Atkinson, like many another, has confused the laws of man with the laws of nature. A law of nature is inexorable, for the simple reason that if it is once broken it is no longer a law of nature, but merely an exploded theory. A human law, on the other hand, is a dead letter unless it has a sanction, whether magical, religious, or social; unless it has some power, human or extra-human, behind it, and unless penalties follow, or are believed to follow, upon its breach. Two men, after taking counsel together, might conceivably enunciate a universally valid law of nature; it is absurd to suppose, even if they were Charlemagne and Harûn ar-Rashîd, and not merely an ape-like creature and his son, that they could promulgate a universally valid human law.

The third, and perhaps most serious, fallacy in that part of Atkinson's theory which we have considered, is that man is naturally jealous. Among all savages divorce is easy and frequent, and as a general rule a wife who is dissatisfied with her husband simply leaves him and takes another. Where a bride-price is paid there may be complications, but they seldom, if ever, take the form of compelling her to return to her husband, who is quite satisfied if the bride-price is repaid, or he receives another woman in exchange. A comparable practice obtains in our divorce courts, where the husband can claim a price from the co-respondent. Among a number of Asiatic and American tribes the woman owns the house, and if she tires of her husband, simply turns him out ; in ancient times this was the rule among the Arabs.

All this is hardly suggestive of the ' woman sacred ' to one savagely jealous man ' theory, and in fact the so-called jealousy of the savage is not due to any objection to his wife's flirtations, but to his fear that she will leave him, and that he will be unable to replace her. Once assured that there is no danger of his wife's being carried off, he is usually quite willing to lend her, while custom often compels him to lend her whether he is willing or not. Innumerable examples could be given, but a few will perhaps suffice.[1]

If the wife of an Eskimo is unable to accompany him on a hunting expedition, he will exchange her for the wife of some man who is staying behind. Among the Cree Indians a ' temporary exchange of wives is not ' uncommon, and the offer of their person is considered ' a necessary part of the hospitality due to strangers '. The men of Easter Island, having learned that the white men had no intention of carrying off their women, pressed them upon visitors with annoying persistence. Among the Australian blacks the old men usually have several wives each, while the young men have none, but there is no pretence of fidelity ; among several of the tribes lovers are formally allotted to all the married women. Throughout British Central Africa infidelity is treated with indifference, according to Sir Harry Johnston, who also tells us that among the Pygmies of the Congo ' adultery does not seem to be ' greatly resented ! ' while among many West African tribes it does not seem to be resented at all. Among the

[1] *Vide* Mothers, II, pp. 99–117.

Mongol tribes of Central Asia ' adultery is not regarded ' as a vice '. The Todas of Southern India ' do not ' appear to comprehend the notion of adultery '. In the New Hebrides, the next group of islands to that in which Atkinson lived and wrote, 'the young men openly make love to the wives of the older men '. In Italy, up to recent years, it was the custom for married women to have *cicisbei*, that is to say, recognized lovers who cohabited with them when their husbands were away. I may add that in England to-day, among certain classes, it is not uncommon for a married woman to have, with her husband's knowledge, what is known as a ' fancy man '.

The foregoing is perhaps sufficient to show that we have no reason to believe that jealousy was the ruling passion with primitive man, and unless it was the ruling passion Atkinson's theory cannot stand.

We may conclude by briefly considering whether what is described as marriage among the more primitive peoples has any claim to be considered as a permanent union. Among many savages there is no marriage ceremony whatever, and in many others the ceremony is of the simplest character, in which, as still in Scotland, the parties have merely to announce their union. Among some of the North American tribes unions are so temporary and informal that what some writers entitle marriage others describe as prostitution. In Persia it is still legal to contract a marriage for one day. It would be easy to adduce ample evidence to show that among the more primitive races the union of the sexes, whether we dignify it with the title of marriage or not, is in general anything but sacred and indissoluble.

JOCASTA'S CRIME

It is, however, interesting to note that in many parts of the world where among the common people adultery is an everyday affair, the slightest familiarity with the wife of a king or chief may be a serious, or even a capital, offence; and this brings us to our last point, which illustrates the developments that are taking place in anthropological thought. Dr. Westermarck[1] notes that 'in some countries the bridegroom and 'bride are regarded as king and queen,' and asks, 'Who would look upon this as a survival from a time 'when marriage was only contracted by royal persons?' obviously expecting the answer 'nobody'; yet a few years later Mr. Hocart[2] was able to write: 'Why 'these royal honours paid to bride and bridegroom? 'The most obvious explanation is that in the countries 'under review marriage is of royal origin: originally 'a ceremony observed by the king and the queen, it 'spread downwards to the lowest classes. . . . Thus 'after all the revolutions in thought that have shaken 'Europe the marriage ceremony still retains the 'impress of its royal origin.'

It would thus appear that a woman becomes sacred to one man not by virtue of any primal law, but only by being, or pretending to be, a queen.

---

[1] *History of Human Marriage*, II, p. 261.
[2] A. M. Hocart, *Kingship*, p. 101.

CHAPTER VII

WAS MARRIAGE BY CAPTURE ONCE GENERAL?

FIFTY years ago the theory that marriage by capture was once general, if not universal, was widely held, and distinguished writers based upon it theories of the origin of exogamy and of the incest taboo. McLennan [1] supposed that early man habitually killed his female children, with the result that women were so scarce that the hordes were obliged to prey upon each other for wives. Herbert Spencer [2] held that female infanticide was less common than McLennan supposed, but that early man was always at war, and that the best warriors captured the most women from other tribes, so that marriage within the tribe became at first dishonourable and later shameful. Lord Avebury's theory [3] was very similar; it was that the women of the tribe were common to the tribe, while captured women belonged to the captors, whose wives they became, so that the women of the tribe were gradually reduced to a spinsterhood from which they could only escape by inducing or permitting some man of another tribe to carry them off.

It would be easy to refute these theories in detail, but it seems unnecessary to do so, since not only are they themselves discredited, but the theory upon which they are based, that which provides a heading for this chapter, has been generally rejected, It is true that Mr. H. G. Wells assures us [4] that 'a young man

[1] J. F. McLennan, *Studies in Ancient History*, pp. 75 seq.
[2] *Principles of Sociology*, I, p. 618. [3] *Origin of Civilization*, p. 114.
[4] *The Work, Wealth and Happiness of Mankind*, p. 43.

'who wanted a woman of his own had to steal her
'from some other group (exogamy)', but it does not
appear that any living anthropologist shares his
opinion.

That marriage by capture has occurred and still
occurs sporadically among many races in many parts
of the world, and at certain times and places has been
fairly common, is undisputed ; that it was never
general seems clear from the fact that no tribe has been
found in which it is the rule ; wherever it occurs, it
occurs as an exception to a regular marriage system. In
the second place, it is clearly incompatible with the
system of matrilocal marriage ; under this system, which
in various forms is found among many peoples
which are low in the scale of civilization and some
which are higher, the husband lives permanently or
for a period at his wife's home, or else lives with his
mother and is merely a visitor to his wife. Traces of
this system are found all over the world, including
England, where the ' wedding breakfast ' is still given
at the bride's home, and there are grounds for the
belief that it was once universal.

While, however, real marriage by capture seems
never to have been customary anywhere, sham marriage
by capture occurs in many parts of the world as a
regular custom, and as this custom is involved in the
suggested solution of the incest problem which will
be put forward later, we shall have to consider it at
some length.

Among the Bushmen of South Africa, when two
young people have agreed to marry, a feast is arranged.
In the middle of the feast the young man seizes his
bride, whereupon all her relatives set about him with

their digging sticks. If he lets go he loses his bride, at any rate for the time. Among the Akamba of East Africa, when a marriage had been arranged, the bridegroom and a party of friends seized the bride in the fields; her brothers sallied out and tried to rescue her, and if they succeeded the bridegroom had to redeem her by paying a larger bride-price. In some parts of Morocco the bride's relatives throw stones at the bridegroom's party. In some parts of Formosa a sham fight takes place between the two families, and it is considered a good omen if blood is drawn. At Chittagong the bride's brother opposes the entrance of the bridegroom, and strikes him seven times with a small stick. In Europe this custom usually takes the form of barricading the road against the bridal procession; in Gloucestershire, as in parts of Burma, the road is barred with a rope, for the removal of which the bridegroom must pay a fee; but in Wales up till recently the bridegroom had to carry off his bride after a mock combat, and a similar custom formerly obtained in Scotland and Ireland.

There are numerous cases in which the bride herself has to put up a strenuous resistance, to run away and at first refuse to be caught, or to feign an exaggerated sorrow, and she has often to display the greatest bashfulness and reluctance, even when, as among the Kamchadals of Siberia, the couple have already cohabited for several years. Among a number of peoples the bride is abducted by the bridegroom's female relatives, while among the Garos of Assam and the Greeks of Macedonia the one to be seized is not the bride but the bridegroom.

Various theories have been proposed to account for

these customs—that they are relics or commemorations of marriage by capture; that they are an expression of genuine sorrow or genuine modesty; that they are tests of the bridegroom's fitness to marry; and finally that they are all magical ceremonies intended to drive off evil spirits.

Dr. Westermarck [1] appears to accept all these theories, though he is unable to follow Crawley [2] in believing that the bride is captured from her sex ' who, ' by psychological necessity, take her part'. It may be possible, but is always improbable, that similar effects should result from dissimilar causes, and I have no doubt that all these customs are the results of the same cause, and that Dr. Karsten, of Helsingfors, was right in believing them to be magical ceremonies.[3]

This theory is discussed by Mr. Briffault [4] and rejected, chiefly on the ground that where there is a bride-price all resistance ends when the bride-price is paid. He also urges a Banyoro custom, by which, though there is no sham fight, yet precautions against violence are taken by disarming the bridal party: ' If simulated violence ', he continues, ' be supposed ' to avert the wrath of evil spirits, it is difficult to ' see how precautions against the occurrence of such ' violence can effect the same purpose.' In some parts of East Africa ritual combats are fought with clubs, and originally these Banyoro may have been deprived of their spears in order to be provided with more appropriate weapons. Whatever may be the case there,

---

[1] From whose *History of Human Marriage*, Vol. II, most of the above examples have been extracted.
[2] Whose *Mystic Rose* we shall meet with later.
[3] R. Karsten, *Studies in South American Anthropology*, I, p. 198.
[4] Mothers, II, pp. 242 seq.

WAS MARRIAGE BY CAPTURE GENERAL? 43

a custom of the Lisus of Burma seems to leave no room for doubt; while the bride is carried off biting and kicking, her relatives cry to the 'ancestral ghost' that they are powerless to keep her.

Mr. Briffault's own theory is that these mock struggles are a commemoration, not of the capture of a bride by hostile tribesmen, but 'of the immemorial 'primitive usage that she should never leave her own 'family and parental abode' even to go to the home of her lawful husband, and he goes on to suggest that the reason why the pretence was persisted in after resistance had ceased to be real was in order to obtain a satisfactory bride-price.

Now while it is possible that matrilocal marriage was once universal, and certain that in many of these cases of mock resistance the bride-price is an important factor, yet it is clear that in most cases either there is no bride-price at all, or it is finally settled before the mock struggle takes place. In all these cases the custom is observed, according to Mr. Briffault's theory, for no reason at all. Now, while people often do things for stupid and insufficient reasons, they never do anything for no reason at all. Customs are always dying out or becoming modified in a way which shows that people observe customs not merely because their fathers observed them, but also because they believe that some benefit accrues from their observance. It is clear that these mock struggles are ritual in character, and when he suggests that they are commemorative, it appears that he has inadequately considered the nature both of commemoration and of ritual. Commemoration is a familiar feature of religion, yet there are two points to be noted: the first is that it is often more than doubtful whether what is commemorative now was commemorative in origin—December the 25th was the sun's birthday long before it was Christmas Day; the second is that where there is genuine commemoration there is always expectation of benefit.

The pious commemorate their patron saints because they believe that the saints have power to help them, and even those who organize centenary festivals would not do so unless they expected to derive some pleasure or profit therefrom. It would be impossible to find in England a sane man, or even a madman, who would plunge an arrow into his eye in order to commemorate the death of King Harold at the Battle of Hastings, yet this is the kind of thing which the savage is supposed to spend his life in doing. In complete defiance of probability he is believed to cause himself endless inconvenience, expense, pain, and humiliation in order to commemorate events long past or practices long extinct without the slightest expectation of receiving any benefit whatever.

We now come to ritual; it will hardly be denied that the customs which we have described are ritual, that is to say, that they consist of a series of acts which must always be performed in exactly the same manner upon the same occasion. Now ritual, though it may rise to become the central feature of a religion, or descend to become a children's game, is invariably and inevitably magical in origin. It is a consequence of the belief, implicit rather than explicit, that man is to such an extent at one with his surroundings that his every word or action produces its effect upon them, and further, that the same words and actions, spoken and performed in the same way, inevitably produce the same reactions. The Moslem belief that Allah likes people to repeat the *fâtiha* a score of times in a day is derived from an older belief that the proper formula, regularly repeated, applies a kind of mechanical stimulus to the universe, and causes it to function in a proper and orderly manner. This again is derived from simpler beliefs, such as that if you want the wind to whistle you must whistle yourself.

A belief, then, in the commemorative nature of ritual argues a misconception of the nature both of commemoration and ritual. A belief that the customs which we are considering are, or are derived from, genuine exhibitions of sorrow or modesty can only be upheld by arbitrarily detaching a selected few of them from their context. We are left with the conclusion that these rites are intended to protect all concerned, but especially the bride and her parents, from supernatural dangers; why these dangers are believed to threaten them will be considered later in connexion with mother-in-law avoidance, and the custom that intercourse between man and wife must take place by stealth.

There still remains one objection of Mr. Briffault's to be considered—why, in cases where there is a brideprice, should the bride's resistance cease as soon as the bride-price is paid? In cases of homicide it is widely believed that the slayer is pursued by the Furies, or by the ghost of the slain, or some other supernatural being; if the slaying is compounded and the bloodmoney paid, the spirits immediately cease from troubling, and there seems to be no reason why they should not be equally accommodating in the case of bride-price.[1]

[1] A parallel between bride-price and blood-money has been suggested by Prof. Radcliffe-Brown (*Man*, 1929, 96), but he ignores the magico-religious aspect.

CHAPTER VIII

DO RELIGIOUS BELIEFS ARISE FROM RATIONAL MEASURES?

ONE of the most surprising things about anthropological literature is the number of utterly unproved assumptions that succeed in passing muster as unquestionable scientific facts. The assumption with which I now propose to deal is that laws based on rational considerations, or arising from sociological developments, sooner or later acquire a supernatural sanction; in other words, that it comes to be believed that such laws were instituted by supernatural authority, and cannot be broken without bringing down dpon the transgressors punishments unconnected with the crime by the ordinary laws of cause and effect.

The theory seems to be—to give a concrete example—that if the law as to dog licences continues in force, people will come to believe that to take out a licence is an infallible means of securing the favour of the Deity or defeating the machinations of the Evil One, and that a dog for which there is no licence in force will inevitably die of distemper.

The theorists, who include almost all the writers on incest origin whom I have quoted or shall quote, do not state a concrete case—in fact, they do not state a case at all. They merely assume, as if it were an obvious fact, that if the members of a tribe were to impose, for whatever reason, incest laws upon themselves, their grandchildren would believe that a breach of these laws would cause displeasure to the

RELIGION AND REASON

supernatural powers, and bring about a famine or a flood.

There are certain facts which seem, at the first glance, to give the theory some support. The Aeneid was composed as a secular poem, but later acquired a quasi-sacred character, and at one time the 'Sortes Vir-'gilianae' were generally regarded as inspired. It must be noted, however, that the poem had descended from a higher culture to a lower, in which it accidentally acquired a religious significance.

Then there are superstitions connected with modern inventions, such as the belief that a witch can only be shot with a silver bullet; such beliefs, however, did not really arise from the inventions with which they are connected, but are merely modifications of prehistoric superstitions.

Every one knows the story of the poor woman with the imbecile daughter, who said, ' I've had her 'vaccinated, and I've had her confirmed, and it don't 'seem to brighten her up a bit,' and this might suggest that vaccination is acquiring a supernatural sanction. This may well be the case, not because it is enforced by law, but because it bears a close resemblance to magical prophylactics of the 'hair of the dog that bit 'him' type.

The theory receives its principal support from, and possibly had its origin in, the attempts which have been made to rationalize the Pentateuch. It has been alleged that Moses was a great sanitarian; that a great part of his code was deliberately enacted from hygienic motives, and that he pretended to have obtained Divine sanction for laws which either were based on the results of his own scientific researches, or were extracted from the regulations issued by the Egyptian Ministry of Health. It has been suggested, for example, that having caused an investigation to be made into the edible properties of Palestinian pork, and found that it was unfit for human consumption, he accordingly forbade the Israelites to eat it. I can say from my own experience that this is quite untrue; the flesh of the Palestinian boar is perfectly sweet and wholesome. Sir James Frazer [1] has dealt with a number of similar fallacies. There is not the slightest justification for basing the Mosaic code upon scientific knowledge, or believing that it was inspired by other than religious ideas.

It is quite common for people to continue to observe, from rational motives, customs which formerly had a supernatural sanction. Many, for example, who no longer anticipate supernatural vengeance for working on the Sabbath, nevertheless observe Sunday as a day of rest for reasons of health. Many people dance Sellenger's Round and similar dances for pleasure, and not to keep the sun on its course. Endless examples could be given, but apart from the deceptive cases which I have mentioned above there seems to be not the slightest evidence for the reverse process, that is to say, for the observance of a law or custom from magico-religious motives after its rational origin had been forgotten.

The earlier theorists made many false assumptions, but there is this to be said in their defence, that they were advancing into completely unexplored country, and without working hypotheses of some kind would have been unable to get along at all. It is not only

[1] FOT, Vol. III.

through the facts which they collected but also through the mistakes which they made that a science of social anthropology is coming into existence. There is less excuse for the more recent writers, some of whom have unfortunately adopted what is known as the 'functional 'system'. The chief tenet held by the followers of this system, and one which makes the scientific study of social origins and developments impossible, is that any one who can invent a plausible excuse for a silly custom has not only justified but completely explained that custom.

It is strange to find Mr. Briffault in such company. Having employed his genius [1] in tracing the progress of mankind from unreason to reason, he has in this case, and apparently in this case only, postulated the reverse process. His theory of incest origin [2] is that the primeval boy, having reached puberty, attempted to rape his younger sister, and that he thereby aroused the jealousy and anger of his mother, who drove him from the family circle to seek female society elsewhere. We are to suppose that the primeval mother had much more leisure to play the duenna than is usual among savage women, and that the chastity of the primeval girl was much more carefully guarded than is that of the savage girl of to-day. Mr. Briffault himself shows that the savage girl usually loses her virginity at a very early age [3] while Professor Malinowski assures [4] us that she is often deflowered by some small boy almost as soon as she can walk.

We can apply to Mr. Briffault his own criticism of Atkinson: [5] 'There appears to be no reason why, the

[1] R. Briffault, *The Making of Humanity.* [2] *Mothers,* I, p. 254.
[3] Ibid., II, pp. 16–64, and III, pp. 312–18.
[4] *Sex and Repression in Savage Society,* p. 55. [5] *Mothers,* I, p. 243, n.

'young males of the group having been driven away, strange males from another group should be admitted.' Finally there is the criticism foreshadowed above—we are to suppose that the youths not only translated their perfectly rational fear of their mothers' heavy hands into a quite irrational horror of supernatural vengeance, but that they impressed this horror upon all the other members of their groups, including the mothers themselves. Alternatively we must suppose that the mothers, who according to Mr. Briffault were the early legislators, found that their hands were not heavy enough, and therefore deliberately called in as a reinforcement a hitherto unimagined supernatural force. It is surely his duty, and that of those who put forward similar theories, to put forward at the same time some evidence to support them.

CHAPTER IX
WAS EARLY MAN A LEGISLATOR?

IT is a widespread belief that the customs and institutions which we find in force among uncivilized peoples are in many, if not in all, cases the result of deliberative legislative action on the part of these people, or of their ancestors; it does not appear, however, that any of the numerous writers on sociological subjects who hold, or seem to hold, this belief have given any thought to the machinery which is necessary if laws are to be passed and enforced. It is impossible in many cases to suppose that the laws are the work of despotic kings or chiefs, for peoples are found in many parts of the world who have, so far as can be ascertained, never had such chiefs, yet whose social organization is no less complex than that of those who have. Our sociologists, however, are for the most part more democratic; they believe that tribes make their own laws. They are not very definite in describing what they suppose actually to happen, but one gathers that in their belief meetings of elders, or warriors, or both, at which new laws, or amendments to old laws, are proposed, discussed, and passed or rejected, are affairs of everyday occurrence.

When, however, we turn to the accounts of those who have made a study of uncivilized peoples we cannot find the slightest grounds for believing that anything of the kind ever happens; tribal councils certainly take place—I have attended them myself—but what they discuss are questions of practical politics, such as whether war should be declared or whether the village ought to be moved. There is no regular procedure ; every one talks at once, and those in favour of one of the alternatives eventually shout down the others.

In these assemblies no question of altering the law ever arises ; nobody, so far as I can ascertain, claims to have heard a tribal council discuss a proposed amendment to the law ; nobody knows of a case in which a tribal law has been amended by a tribal council. Cases of course occur in which tribal laws are modified by external pressure, as when the paramount power forbids human sacrifice, or a cattle plague makes it impossible to continue paying the bride-price in cattle ; but even in such cases there is no evidence that the laws are ever formally altered. What seems to happen is that the new state of affairs is at first regarded as a makeshift, but that gradually the old state of affairs is forgotten, and the new law takes up its tacit position among the immemorial usages of the tribe. We find, at any rate, that the great majority of peoples, both savage and civilized, believe that their law has come down to them, in the form in which it now is, from the distant past, and that the prosperity of the country depends entirely upon its strict observance.[1] Alteration is, as a rule, unthought of and unthinkable ; ' the laws of the Medes and Persians, which cannot be ' altered ', the *nolimus leges Angliae mutare* of the English barons, are not isolated instances of extreme conservatism, but are typical of the universal attitude of mankind.

---

[1] In every native community the force of tradition is stronger than among ourselves. . . . Any departure from old teaching was strongly disapproved of.—R. Firth, *Primitive Economics of the New Zealand Maori*, pp. 152, 177.

WAS EARLY MAN A LEGISLATOR?

Let us leave Europe for the moment and return to the savage. We have seen that the idea of making even the smallest alteration in his law never occurs to the modern savage, and in considering how he got his law we must suppose either :

(1) That the mentality of his ancestors was totally different from his own ; or
(2) That the law was imposed by some individual of exceptional ability and character ; or
(3) That is was imposed by necessity following changes in environmental conditions ; or
(4) That it is the result of a process of gradual and unconscious development.

In my own view, as I have already indicated, the last alternative is the correct one, but it may be as well to show the improbability of the others. As regards the first, while the culture of the savage may have advanced, there is not the slightest evidence that the essential features of his mentality, or indeed of human mentality in general, are different from what they were five thousand or fifty thousand years ago. Let us take for example the Ashanti, whose law is extremely detailed and comprehensive ; there is no justification for supposing that at some time in the past their ancestors accepted a brand-new code of laws covering every aspect of their lives, endowed it with a sacrosanct character, and immediately sank into a state of extreme and permanent conservatism.

Let us now take the all-powerful lawgiver ; he is usually a myth, but when a real person turns out to be not a law-maker, but merely a law-spreader. Let us quote Mr. Leonard Woolley on Hammurabi. He says :[1] 'The only arbitrary feature in Hammurabi's 'code is the application to the whole empire of laws 'whose origin had been local and their vogue restricted.' It could be shown that these remarks apply equally to all the lawgivers of history, and must therefore be presumed to apply to all the lawgivers of pre-history.

We now come to the third alternative. It might be supposed that early codes were conditioned by the struggle for existence, that is to say, that those communities which adopted, by whatever machinery, certain laws, were enabled to obtain the most food with the least difficulty, while protecting themselves adequately against cold and disease, against anarchy within and enemies without, whereas those communities which failed to adopt such laws perished miserably. It could no doubt be shown that communities have adapted their laws, gradually and unconsciously, to altered conditions of food supply, but as a general proposition the theory that the laws of a community are in the nature of a response to its environment will not stand a moment's investigation.

Let us take the almost universal practice of trial by ordeal. We find communities in which it is harmless and others which have almost exterminated themselves by means of it.[2] Then take circumcision, which in various forms is inflicted on both sexes in many parts of the world. There is no question of response to environment; on the whole the advantage is with those who do not practise this mutilation, which in some of its forms may result in the death of the victim; but we find circumcised and uncircumcised communities living side by side, both in Europe and Central

[1] C. L. Woolley, *The Sumerians*, p. 92.   [2] GB, IV, p. 197.

Africa, and enjoying equal health and prosperity. Or take the laws as to the disposal of the dead, which occupy an important place in most codes, both civilized and savage ; it is impossible to suppose that the Parsees, for example, were induced by environmental conditions to expose their dead on towers, or have by so doing been either helped or hindered in the struggle for existence.

Far from adapting his laws to his needs, man spends his life in trying to adapt himself to his laws, and often perishes in the attempt.

Though, even in civilized communities, deliberate changes in the ancient and fundamental laws are very seldom made, yet in all communities change is always taking place. The reason is that, so long as the laws are unwritten, those responsible for memorizing the laws are always liable to be unconsciously influenced by the circumstances of the time ; a higher material culture may be leading to a more enlightened morality ; the ideas of more civilized neighbours may be creeping in ; new knowledge may be making the old ideas seem absurd—sometimes the elders or priests will be influenced by these developments and sometimes they will not, but change will gradually come. Even when the law is written, changes come about in a similar manner ; the law is, of course, sacred and unalterable, but the language in which it is written gradually becomes archaic, and it is amplified or modified by commentaries which though less sacred are more intelligible, till they in their turn become archaic.

In the lower cultures, then, deliberate changes are never made in the law ; all law arises and develops through a process of gradual evolution; this may seem a hazardous position to take up, but I shall endeavour to defend it with some historical examples. If savages can deliberately alter their laws, it might be supposed that our Nordic ancestors would have had this power, but it seems clear that they had not. Du Chaillu[1] tells us that the law of Norway contained no provision for altering the law. The Thing, whose sole, or at any rate chief, business was the settling of lawsuits, was bound by the decision of the Lawman, whose position was very similar to that of a Moslem *mufti*. He had to know the law by heart, and to swear to hand it on as he had received it. He received a salary for performing certain duties, such as drawing up the calendar, and was bound, on payment of his fee, to declare the law on any particular point to any one who consulted him.

What actually happened we may learn from the account given in the *Saga of Burnt Njal*[2] of the conversion of Iceland to Christianity. During the last years of the tenth century missionaries from Norway had made many converts among the leading men, and when the Althing met in June A.D. 1000 civil war seemed imminent. A Christian convert who had been exiled for blaspheming the gods rode to the Thing escorted by a large body of armed Christians, and the pagans also came armed; both sides declared themselves out of each others' laws, and all was shouting and confusion. In these circumstances Hall of the Side, a chief who had been converted to Christianity and a man of peace, took a momentous step: he went to Thorgeir the Lawman, who was a

[1] *The Viking Age*, I, p. 536.   [2] Chapter CI.

pagan, and paid him his fee of three marks of silver to utter the law.

'Thorgeir lay all that day on the ground, and spread 'a cloak over his head, so that no man spoke with him; 'but the day after men went to the Hill of Laws, and 'then Thorgeir bade them be silent and listen, and 'spoke thus—" It seems to me as though our matters '" were come to a deadlock, if we are not all to have '" one and the same law; for if there be a sundering '" of laws, then there will be a sundering of the '" peace, and we shall never be able to live in the '" land. Now I will ask both Christian men and '" heathen whether they will hold to those laws which '" I utter ".'

They all gave pledges that they would, and he then said: 'This is the beginning of our laws, that all men 'shall be Christians here in the land, and believe in 'one God, the Father, the Son, and the Holy Ghost, 'but leave off all idol-worship, not expose children to 'perish, and not eat horseflesh. It shall be outlawry 'if such things are proved openly against any man; 'but if these things are done by stealth, then it shall 'be blameless.'

I have quoted this account at some length because it shows that nothing was further from the minds of the Icelanders, although they were by no means savages, and although they were republicans, than the idea of amending the law by discussion and vote. The law could not be altered, even to avoid civil war, except by deliberate perjury on the part of the Lawman.

Things were much the same in England; it is often alleged that the *witanagemot* had wide powers of legislation, but if it had such powers, which is doubtful, it certainly did not exercise them, for at the Norman Conquest there was no general law in existence in England. 'There were the Mercian law, the Dane 'law, and the West Saxon law. They all varied in 'their contents—indeed if their provisions were the 'same on any given point such agreement was thought 'worthy of note, and within these three districts the 'customs of localities varied.'[1]

As the last part of this chapter will be devoted to a criticism of Sir James Frazer's theory of incest origin, which is based on the belief that man is naturally a legislator, it will be appropriate to draw from his own works a further illustration of the fact that man is not naturally a legislator. He assures us,[2] and cites many eminent scholars in support of his opinion, that the thirty-fourth chapter of Exodus contains the original version of the Ten Commandments. The differences between this version and that with which we are more familiar are striking; the prohibitions of murder, theft, and adultery are absent, and their place is taken by purely ritual prohibitions, such as ' the fat of my feast shall not remain all night ' until the morning '.

If Sir James and his authorities are right, it is impossible to believe that this is a case of deliberate legislation, that is, that one set of commandments was deliberately substituted for the other. In the first place it seems certain that any person, or body of persons, intending a deliberate substitution would have omitted, or at any rate amended, the chapter in question; in the second place we must take into

[1] W. S. Holdsworth, *History of English Law*, I, p. 3.
[2] FOT, III, p. 111.

WAS EARLY MAN A LEGISLATOR? 59

account the extremely conservative character of the Jews. As Josephus puts it :[1] ' We think it to be the 'most necessary business of our whole life, to observe 'the laws that have been given us, and to keep those 'rules of piety which have been handed down to us.' The universality of this sentiment, at any rate in the lower cultures, should suffice to acquit the Jews of the charge of being a peculiar people ; we may be sure that any change in their law was made gradually and unconsciously.

That people can alter the laws under which they live was a discovery of the Greeks. At Sparta the very primitive code ascribed to Lycurgus was sacred and unalterable, like all early codes,[2] but in some of the other city-states, notably Athens, the popular assemblies which were held periodically for such purposes as electing officials or deciding questions of peace and war developed gradually, under the influence of the philosophers, into legislative bodies, though the suspicion with which attempts to change the law continued to be regarded is shown by such provisions as that at Thurii, by which any one proposing a new law had to do so with a halter round his neck, ready to be hanged if his law failed to pass.

From Greece the idea eventually reached Western Europe, but it is still completely foreign to the majority of the human race. With these facts in mind let us now consider the views of Sir James Frazer, the most distinguished of those writers who attribute the origin of the incest taboo, or rather the origin of its enforcement, to deliberate legislation.

In his *Totemism and Exogamy*[3] Sir James concludes

[1] *Against Apion*, I, 12. [2] Plutarch, *Lycurgus*. [3] Vol. IV, p. 169.

that mankind was originally promiscuous, but that the growth of some superstition, the nature of which cannot even be conjectured, led them to object to the marriage of near kin, and they devised the system of exogamy to prevent such marriages. In his *Folklore in the Old Testament* [1] he goes further, for he tells us that ' all the evidence points to the conclusion that ' the dual organization, or division of a community ' into two exogamous and intermarrying classes, was ' introduced for the purpose of preventing the marriage ' of brothers and sisters, which presumably had ' hitherto been lawful, though no doubt the feeling ' against it had been growing long before it took ' definite shape in the dual organization. That organi- ' zation, which may be described as the first great ' moral reformation of which we have any record, ' absolutely prevented these objectionable unions for ' the future by the very simple expedient of assigning ' all the brothers and sisters of a family to the same ' exogamous class, and prohibiting marriages between ' members of the same exogamous class '. What Sir James does not realize is that exogamy depends, and must necessarily depend, on barring marriage between persons related, however remotely, through one sex, and disregarding relationship through the other sex. In a non-exogamous community, on the other hand, whatever restrictions there are on the marriage of kin, it must inevitably happen that every one is related to every one else, either closely or remotely, through both sexes. It would be easy to assign all the brothers and sisters of a family to Group A, but the next step would be to assign all their husbands and wives to

[1] Vol. II, p. 233.

Group B, and it would then be found that the latter were all related to each other and must go into different groups. The further the scheme went the greater would be the confusion, and it would be found that far from being a 'very simple expedient' it would be quite impossible to carry it out unless all existing relationships were completely disregarded. It is difficult to explain this clearly and concisely, but any one who takes the trouble to try to divide his connexions, or the inhabitants of his village, into two exogamous classes, will find that what I say is true. It is strange that Sir James should have fallen into this mistake, since he realizes the prevalence of cross-cousin marriage and its importance as showing that exogamy arose through the division of groups and not through their fusion. We shall examine this question later, and I shall try to show that exogamy must date from a time before marriage existed, or paternity was recognized.

Sir James bases his conclusions largely on the researches of Sir Baldwin Spencer and Mr. Gillen among the natives of Central Australia; but while the facts adduced by these writers must command the greatest respect, their conclusions do not always seem justified. They state that the Australians are ruled by councils of old men; that these councils have the power to make such a change as the introduction of exogamy, and that their ability to devise such a system is shown by the ease with which they unravel the intricacies of the existing systems. This seems to commit them, or at any rate to commit Sir James, who appears to have gone rather beyond them, to the theory that any one who can use a table of logarithms is a potential Napier.

Sir James really supplies the refutation of his own theory when he says :[1] 'Indeed some tribes which 'discountenance the marriage of first cousins never 'advanced beyond the stage of the two class system. 'This shows how even an exogamous community 'may by a simple prohibition bar marriages which it 'disapproves of without needing to extend its exo- 'gamous system by further subdivision', and *a fortiori* how a non-exogamous community could bar marriages which it disapproved of without resorting to exogamy at all. Since, however, as we have seen, savages never legislate, the prohibition cannot be as simple as Sir James supposes. There is ample evidence to show that the laws of these Australian tribes are not of their own devising, but that, perhaps two or three thousand years ago, they were strongly but temporarily influenced by people of a much higher culture.

It is regrettable that in this case Sir James did not follow his usual practice of fortifying his argument by example ; had he attempted to do so, he could hardly have written :[2] 'Doubtless it would be a mistake to 'imagine that the formal introduction of that system '(exogamy) made a great and sudden break. . . . 'That is not the way in which legislative changes are 'effected either in savage or in civilized society. . . . 'The new law simply renders obligatory and universal 'a practice which had before been optional,' for he would have been led to suspect, from the silence of the writers whom he consulted, that changes in savage law do not come about as he supposes. To quote an old but judicious writer :[3] ' We suspect indeed that

---

[1] *Totemism and Exogamy*, IV, p. 120.   [2] FOT, II, p. 235.
[3] C. Thirlwall, *History of Greece*, I, p. 296.

WAS EARLY MAN A LEGISLATOR?

'this opinion rests on a false notion of the omnipotence 'of human legislators, which has always been preva- 'lent among philosophers, but has never been con- 'firmed by experience.'

I should not like to close this chapter on a note of criticism. Sir James Frazer has realized that the incest taboo could only have originated in 'some superstition'; he has seen that exogamy must have been due to division within the group, and could not have come from marriage by capture or an alliance between tribes; and finally, he has provided us with the material wherewith to refute his own theory. One can only regret the lack of some personal familiarity with savage life, which would have made his great works still greater.

CHAPTER X
WAS EARLY MAN A SOCIAL REFORMER?

WE must now consider the theories of certain present-day social anthropologists, theories based on the belief, which we have in the last chapter shown to be false, that there are grounds for crediting our early ancestors with a passion for social reform. Let us begin with Dr. R. R. Marett, who tells us [1] that 'within the (primitive) domestic
' group there are fundamental laws to be observed,
' such as notably three : to avoid sexual relations with
' group-mates ; to avoid killing them ; and if they
' are killed by outsiders to kill these in turn. These
' three laws of the blood are so engrained in the moral
' nature of the savage that one is tempted to overlook
' their social origin, which must be traced back to
' very early insistence on the domestic proprieties,
' possibly on the part of the mothers whose blood was
' the symbol of social decency and honour. . . . It
' is probably quite wrong to imagine the primitive
' horde as essentially a harem owned and guarded by
' an ever-jealous patriarch—a sort of Grand Turk.
' With just as much, if not more, right could one
' compose a myth of Amazons who are economically
' self-sufficient enough to be able likewise to retain
' the initiative in the bestowal of their favours. Using
' their authority to stop in the young what they could
' not so well prevent in the old, they might at length
' succeed in putting their ban—one might almost say

[1] *An Outline of Modern Knowledge*, pp. 406 and 413.

WAS EARLY MAN A SOCIAL REFORMER? 65

'their curse—alike on mating and fighting within the
'home-circle. Given the proximity of more or less
'related and friendly bands, there would be no great
'hardship in obliging the young men to go abroad
'on amorous visits, especially when it was understood
'by their neighbours that the compliment could be
'returned'. We must be careful to note that when
Dr. Marett speaks of the 'domestic proprieties' he
is referring to early man and not to Early Victorian
man. I shall refer to his views on myth and symbolism
in a later chapter, and shall forbear to criticize his
theory till we have considered that of Mrs. Seligman,
which is very similar.

She tells us[1] that 'a sexual relationship between
'parent and child would be dangerous to the family
'group . . . for the child would then be raised to the
'social level of the parent. From this point of view
'intercourse of father and daughter would upset . . .
'the group just as much as intercourse of the son
'with the mother. . . . It is important to remember
'this, for most theories of incest deal only with the
'jealousies that would arise between father and son.
'While it is easy to see that in the absence of a law
'with supernormal sanction the father would prevail
'and prevent such intercourse until the son reached
'maturity, and that he in turn would show no pity
'to the father, it has never been shown how a woman
'could prevent intercourse between her husband and
'her own daughter, nor indeed why such intercourse
'should appear in so heinous a light, since no objection
'is made in savage society by a middle-aged woman
'to her husband taking another wife as young as her

[1] JRAI, 1929, pp. 243 seq.

'own daughter. But if the prohibition of incest is
'looked upon as a social law regulating the behaviour
'of an entire social group (the family) rather than as a
'rule which gives old men sanction for checking the
'desires of their sons, the avoidance of both types of
'parent-child incest can be understood as safeguards
'to parental authority. . . . If a social law can be
'accepted which at the same time protects the mother
'from the son and the daughter from the father, the
'authority of both parents can be maintained. The
'father keeps his authority over the family by accepting
'a rule which deprives him of intercourse with his
'daughter. In doing so the father gives up a real
'advantage, for there can be no doubt that very young
'girls are attractive to mature men . . . while the sons
'only further repressed what was already a phantasy.
'It is unlikely, then, that the fathers would allow the
'sons so easy a triumph by allowing them to take the
'daughters, for, towards them, father and son are again
'rivals. . . . The two incest taboos are thus comple-
'mentary to one another and together eliminate certain
'possible sources of disharmony within the group'.

We have already considered[1] Professor Malinowski's theory in its main outlines, but may note here that he carries the belief that early man was obsessed with a passion for social reform to greater lengths even than Dr. Marett and Mrs. Seligman, for while they seem to admit the possibility of some cultural progress before the imposition of the incest taboo, he will have none of it: 'Incest must be forbidden
'because . . . incest is incompatible with the estab-
'lishment of the first foundations of culture.'

[1] In Chapter III.

It would be easy to criticize such theories in detail, but most of the points have already been covered. We have seen that while among ourselves the incest taboo works bilaterally, among savages, with certain exceptions which we shall discuss later, it works unilaterally; we have seen that among savages incest is neither a moral sin nor a social misdemeanour, but a national catastrophe; we have seen that early man had no idea of paternity; that exogamy could not possibly have arisen in a society in which individual marriage in any form existed; that rational laws never acquire supernatural sanction, and that savages never legislate. I have perhaps stated these facts more dogmatically than the evidence warrants, but they, and others which we shall come to later, are the relevant facts, and no theorist who fails to take them into account can be considered to have more than touched the fringe of the subject. Not only have the writers whom I have just quoted failed to take these facts into account, but they have also failed to realize the revolutionary character of the changes which they postulate. We are apparently asked to picture a district, or a continent, sparsely inhabited by groups of hunters. Each group lives in a state of sexual communism; the members of a group may snarl over the last morsel of carrion; they may elbow each other away from the lee side of the fire; two males may occasionally come to blows because they desire intercourse with the same female at the same time; but they must have reached a *modus vivendi*, or they would have ceased to exist. Suddenly their whole social organization is completely altered; what has been right becomes abominable; what has been undreamed of becomes right. If the people of England were suddenly to decide to abandon family life and have their wives in common, the change would be less drastic, since it would merely involve the breaking down of social barriers, a far simpler matter than setting them up.

What was the motive which induced these primeval savages to make this revolutionary change, and sacrifice themselves thus upon the altar of the unknown future? Dr. Marett and Professor Malinowski do not tell us, but according to Mrs. Seligman it was a desire to 'eliminate certain possible sources of 'disharmony within the group'. There are many possible sources of disharmony within the group in England to-day, which are remediable but which are not remedied: was early man so much more enlightened and far-sighted than we are? We cannot believe that he was.

Let us conclude with what is perhaps the strongest argument against the theories of these distinguished writers; they share with the lowest savages the belief that the accidental and temporary features of their own local culture (the 'domestic proprieties') are inevitable, eternal, and universal.

'The whole study of social psychology will have
'to be ordered on different lines in the future if any
'progress is to be made. The facile habit of inventing
'pictures of early times will have to be abandoned in
'favour of the method of relying solely on facts,
'however unpalatable they may be. It will have to
'be realized that civilized men, in their actions, afford
'but little evidence of those of their forerunners, that
'in the course of the development of civilization

'entire transformations may have taken place in 'human behaviour', says Dr. Perry,[1] and I have no doubt that he is right. It cannot be too strongly emphasized that the theories which I have discussed in this chapter, as well as those which I shall discuss in the next, have not the slightest atom of evidence to support them.

---

[1] W. J. Perry, *The Children of the Sun*, p. 239.

CHAPTER XI
FREUD'S THEORIES

MOST of the criticisms which are applicable to the theories outlined in the last chapter apply equally to Freud's theories; but since these theories have acquired a certain vogue, it is perhaps desirable to consider them separately.

It would appear that Freud, being rightly convinced of the importance of his psycho-analytical theories, and not unnaturally anxious to try them out on a larger stage than that afforded by the neurotic members of the Viennese *bourgeoisie*, put himself through a course of the works of Sir James Frazer. He then wrote a series of essays which were later published in book form under the title of *Totem and Taboo*; they consist for the most part of long extracts from Frazer's writings, followed by short comparisons with or illustrations from the theories of psycho-analysis, and seem to have been originally intended merely as suggestions for a possible understanding between psycho-analysis and anthropology.

In them he puts forward two different, and indeed contradictory, theories of the origin of the incest taboo. The first is that certain early fathers, while continuing to commit incest themselves, imposed, for some unexplained reason, the incest taboo upon their sons, and that the latter, following the precept rather than the example of their fathers, religiously observed the taboo, and passed it on to their children. Thus he tells us[1] that ' there are grounds for assuming that the

[1] p. 8, n.

FREUD'S THEORIES

'totem prohibitions are directed first of all against
'the incestuous desires of the son', and later [1] that
'taboos are very ancient prohibitions which at one
'time were forced upon a generation of primitive
'people from without, that is, they probably were
'impressed upon them by an earlier generation'. The
father who, cigarette in mouth, tries to impress upon
his son the evils of smoking is doomed to failure, as
Freud would have realized had he paused to think.
He did not do so, apparently because at this point
he chanced upon Atkinson's *Primal Law* [2] and at once
took it to his bosom, while his earlier theory passed
out of his mind, though not out of his book.

The touch of psycho-analysis, however, has brought
about a change comparable to that wrought by Circe's
magic cup; instead of the affecting, if impossible, scene
of mother-love triumphant with which Atkinson
regales us, we are introduced to a horrible tragedy of
parricide, cannibalism, and remorse. 'One day the
'expelled brothers joined forces, slew and ate the
'father, and thus put an end to the father horde. . . .
'They hated the father who stood so powerfully in
'the way of their sexual demands and their desire for
'power, but they also loved and admired him. After
'they had satisfied their hate by his removal, and had
'carried out their wish for identification with him, the
'suppressed tender impulses had to assert themselves.
'This took place in the form of remorse, a sense of
'guilt was formed which coincided here with the
'remorse generally felt. . . . They undid their deed
'by declaring that the killing of the father substitute,
'the totem, was not allowed, and renounced the fruits

[1] p. 52. [2] With which we dealt in Chapter VI.

'of the deed by denying themselves the liberated women. Thus they created the two fundamental taboos of totemism out of the sense of guilt of the son, and for this very reason these had to correspond with the two repressed wishes of the Oedipus complex. Whoever disobeyed became guilty of the two only [sic] crimes which troubled primitive society.'[1]

One would like to know what happened next; the wording of the passage suggests that there was only one horde, in which case both the parricidal sons and the 'liberated women' would have had nothing to look forward to but a life of celibacy; if, on the other hand, there were other father hordes, then one parricide could not put an end to the father horde. Freud was far too pleased to find a theory of human origins to which he could affiliate his Oedipus complex to be troubled by any such difficulties, and the combined theory having taken its place as one of the dogmas of the psycho-analytic faith, it is not permissible for his followers to do more than try to find arguments in its support. Yet the difficulties in the way of its acceptance are insuperable. The whole theory depends on the hypothesis that as soon as the sons had killed their father, a capacity for feeling remorse was suddenly conferred upon them, 'a sense of guilt was formed'. But feelings of guilt and remorse only arise in connexion with the fear of punishment, and then only if the subject believes that he has made a wrong choice. The civilized man often feels remorse because he owes a variety of allegiances—to his family, his friends and neighbours, the members of his trade or profession, the law, his country and his religion—all

[1] Op. cit., pp. 235–8.

of which make different and often conflicting demands upon him. It is in the mental strain set up by these conflicting demands that feelings of guilt and remorse have their origin. The savage has no such feelings, since for him there is normally no conflict; he never intentionally breaks the tribal taboos, since they are the only code to which he owes allegiance; and since he has been brought up in their observance, they cause him no anxiety. Should he happen to break one of these taboos, he feels no remorse, but accepts the consequences with the same feelings as he would the consequences of accidentally breaking his leg.

The idea of penance is even further removed from savage mentality, since it is wholly dependent on a belief in purgatory. It consists in undergoing a lesser punishment now in the hope of avoiding a greater punishment later. What applies to the modern savage must apply much more strongly to early man, who had not only no idea of penance, but had by hypothesis not yet arrived at the taboo stage, so that when Freud credits him with ideas of remorse and penance, he is guilty of what has been well termed a psychological anachronism.

Freud's beliefs that savages regard their totems as 'fathers substitute' and parricide as the most appalling of crimes are quite unfounded. In so far as they can be said to regard the totem as a relative at all, it is as a brother rather than as a father; and parricide, far from being universally regarded as a crime, is among many peoples a duty. Frazer[1] gives examples from South America and Siberia of tribes in which the old people are habitually killed by their sons or other

---

[1] GB, IV, p. 14.

relatives, quotes Procopius on a similar practice among the ancient Teutons, and tells us, on the authority of Grimm, that 'the Wends used to kill 'their aged parents and other kinsfolk, and having 'killed them they boiled and ate their bodies'. He concludes that the practice may once have been common to the whole Aryan stock; but since, in addition to the cases he mentions, similar customs have been reported from Kurdistan, Central Africa, and Polynesia, we may well believe that it was once universal. If this was the case it would follow that Freud's hypothetical sons, far from committing an unprecedented crime, were merely anticipating what would shortly have become their duty.

Let us now turn to the central feature of the whole system, the Oedipus complex—that every boy is subconsciously obsessed with a desire to kill his father and marry his mother. There seems to be no doubt that this complex occurs among European neurotics, and it may occur to some extent among normal Europeans; but even Freud's own followers have been unable to find it among savages, and have been reduced to the necessity of postulating a repressed repression in order to account for its apparent absence. It seems clear, however, that this complex, where it exists, is one of the numerous consequences of the simultaneous stimulation and repression of the sexual impulse which is one of the features of our social system. Among the classes from which Freud drew his data, women often retain their sexual attractiveness until after their sons have reached puberty. Wherever a boy looks, whether in real life, in pictures, in books, or on the stage, scenes of sexual passion are thrust upon his sight and his imagination; yet the only woman whom he may kiss and fondle is his mother, so that he is liable to fall in love with his mother, and to be envious of his father, who has a prior claim on her attentions. Among savages, on the other hand, women age rapidly, and the result of this, combined with the low birth-rate and high infantile death-rate, is that by the time a boy reaches puberty his mother is normally a withered hag. He is usually, if not invariably, allowed opportunities for sexual gratification elsewhere, with the result that he no more thinks of falling in love with his mother than a young married European does of falling in love with his grandmother.

There is a universal tendency to suppose that any trait which is common among people whom we know is characteristic of the entire human race, but a nerve-specialist is no more entitled to assume that the neuroses which he finds among his patients were found among early mankind than is the chiropodist to assume that early man was a martyr to corns.

CHAPTER XII

IS THE INCEST TABOO MAGICAL IN ORIGIN?

AT a later stage the view will be put forward that incest was originally nothing but a breach of the law of exogamy, that exogamy was adopted for purely magical reasons, and that we are in a position, not to state definitely how and why it was adopted, but to point out pretty clearly the line of investigation which must be followed if an answer to these questons is to be found. At this stage all that will be done is to mention those writers who have suggested a magico-religious origin for the incest taboo.

As we have seen, Sir James Frazer attributes it to 'the growth of some superstition'. Andrew Lang wrote:[1] 'To be sinful, endogamy within the group 'must have offended some superstitious belief . . . 'incest, among the young, is really prevented by the 'religious horror with which, by most peoples, it is 'regarded.' Dr. Raymond Firth writes of the people of Tikopia in the Solomon Islands:[2] 'It is 'the native belief that such marriages [*sc.* between 'near kin] are bound to be sterile, and definite instances 'are given in support of this generalization. This 'looks at first as though the Tikopians had formulated 'on empirical evidence some biological principle as 'to the evil effects of inbreeding. Their reasoning, 'however, is not at all of the scientific order, but 'belongs to the realm of religious belief . . . (it) 'rests on a basis of supernaturalism.'

[1] *Social Origins*, pp. 23, 26.   [2] JRAI, 1930, p. 248.

THE INCEST TABOO AND MAGIC

The only writer who, so far as I can learn, has definitely suggested a magical origin for the incest taboo is the late Professor Durkheim, of Paris, and his essay[1] is a valuable contribution to the study of the problem. His views as to how the practice of exogamy arose are well-considered; he rightly scorns the idea that such institutions were deliberately introduced for preconceived purposes, and rejects the idea that the incest taboo is instinctive. He concludes that the basis of the taboo is purely magical, and attributes it to a belief that a man who married a virgin of his own totemic clan shed the blood of the totemic god, and thereby incurred his implacable resentment. A man of another clan is, however, outside the 'sphere of 'action' of the totem, and can therefore shed its blood with impunity.[2]

Professor Durkheim is one of the few writers on this subject who have tried to find a theory which would cover the facts, instead of following the usual practice of taking one particular incest law, real or imaginary, devising a theory which might account for it, and ignoring all facts which do not fit in with the theory. It is, however, some thirty-five years since he wrote, and we now know a great deal more about savages than we did then. We know, for example, that the totem is not, as was formerly supposed, always an important animal; it may be a plant, a small bird, or even an artificial object, and though it must be treated with respect, or at any rate with caution, it is never regarded as in any sense a god. Another fact which we have learned is that among nearly all savages prenuptial chastity is unknown, so that while the rupture

[1] In *L'Année Sociologique*, Vol. I. [2] Op. cit., pp. 15, 38, 94.

of the hymen is of great magical importance among peoples of higher culture, such as the Arabs, and while the rite is in all probability associated with the group of ideas and practices which gave rise to the incest taboo, it can itself hardly have had a share in the inception of that taboo.

Professor Durkheim's theory was intended to cover the origin not only of the incest taboo, but also of the dual organization, and this leads us to another objection. It would seem that the theory could only be sustained if every tribe was divided, before the institution of the dual organization, into two, and not more than two, totemic clans. It seems probable to me that the dual organization is a consequence of the fact that there are two sexes, and a result of exogamy, but of this more anon.

CHAPTER XIII

OTHER THEORIES

PROFESSOR Elliot Smith[1] tells us that 'there 'was no one except the king's own sister of 'celestial rank fit to be the mother of a king. 'Hence the apotheosis of the king has as one of 'its many strange results the inauguration of the 'practice of incest as the approved marriage of a 'ruler. As this procedure was regarded as the king's 'divine right, a practice devised to meet his special 'circumstances as a divine being, it was made the 'most heinous offence on the part of the common 'people to imitate his actions in this respect. Hence 'in all the earliest forms of civilized society the severest 'penalties are imposed upon those who have sexual 'relations within the forbidden limits of relationship 'imposed by law and custom'. He says nothing of savage society, and it is not clear whether he supposes that exogamy, wherever it exists, originated in the manner which he suggests. If that is his theory, and if that theory were the correct one, we should confidently expect to find the incest taboo, and especially the taboo on marriage between brother and sister, most stringently enforced in those countries in which the idea of divine kingship reached its highest development, and non-existent in those countries in which there is no trace of divine kingship.

What we actually find is the reverse ; nowhere has the idea of divine kingship been more highly developed

[1] *Human History*, p. 306.

than among the ancient Egyptians, yet there seems to be no doubt that marriage between brother and sister was common among them from very early times, and became commoner as time went on, so much so that Mr. Briffault tells us [1] that ' so habitual was the usage 'that even as late as the second century A.D. unions ' between brothers and sisters constituted in some ' districts the great majority of the marriages'. On the other hand, while it cannot be said that the evidence for traces of divine kingship among the Australian blacks is very strong, the union of a brother and sister is regarded by them with a horror which is unsurpassed in any part of the world. If we take the ancient Persians on the one hand and the Eskimo on the other, we arrive at a similar result. The evidence seems to suggest that the universal tendency of the ruled to imitate the rulers is as well exemplified in the laws of incest as it is, according to Mr. Hocart, in the marriage ceremonies.

Mr. A. E. Crawley thought that the incest taboo was a purely religious idea, and an extension of the general taboo on relations between the sexes; but he did not explain what he meant by religious, and the reasons he gives for this extension are impossible to follow. He says [2] that there is a ' subconscious or ' conscious " aversion " to love and marriage, first ' between those who are in continuous contact, and ' secondly, between those who are not '. He goes on to say that the incest taboo is due to the fact that brothers and sisters are separated and are therefore strangers, and as such taboo to each other, and also

---

[1] Mothers, I, p. 384, where numerous authorities are cited.
[2] *The Mystic Rose*, II, p. 208.

OTHER THEORIES

to the fact that they are not separated, and are therefore intimates, and as such taboo to each other!

The following older theories are taken from Huth.[1] They do not call for detailed comment, but are interesting as showing the straits in which those who have attempted to account for the incest taboo have found themselves, and also the newness of the idea, in Europe at any rate, that the marriage of near kin results in defective children.

Socrates objected to such marriages that they generally took place between an old man and a young woman, as in the case of marriage of uncle and niece. Plato maintained, as did afterwards Novatian, that they are contrary to the law of nature; he adds that else every one would marry those whom they most resembled, and there would be no proper mixture of characters and property. Aristotle feared that love would become immoderate if, to the usual ties of paternal or fraternal love, marital love were superadded. Chrysippus and Zeno considered every prohibition, though between the nearest relatives, as absurd; but Philo, Agathias, and Statius thought that the respect that we owe to a father should preclude all thought of marriage with his wife. Plutarch took a more matter-of-fact view: who would a wife have to complain to when her husband beat her if their parents were the same? St. Chrysostom adopts the view of Aristotle, and asks, 'Are there not ties of 'love enough between relatives, that you should seek 'to draw them tighter by marriage to the exclusion 'of the rest of mankind?' St. Augustine took a similar view; marriage between near kin would

[1] Op. cit., pp. 149 seq.

prevent the extension of kindred, and therewith charity. He considered that the marriage of Adam's children among themselves was not reprehensible, but it would have been wrong if their sons had married sisters instead of first cousins. Marriages between first cousins are not unlawful, yet they are so near to that which is unlawful that he is glad to see them discouraged. Lastly 'there is a certain laudable 'natural instinct in a man's shamefastness to abstain 'from using that lust upon such as propinquity hath 'bound him chastely to respect'. Like some modern writers, he sees no need to explain why man must forbid what nature has already forbidden.

Pope Gregory I believed that marriages between near kin were sterile. Thomas Aquinas held that all persons who lived under the same roof were forbidden to intermarry, since were they allowed to do so this liberty would violently inflame their passions. These prohibitions had been further extended by the spiritual law, because men must be debarred from carnal things to the end that they may rather attach themselves to spiritual matters. Luther's view was the opposite of that of Aristotle and St. Chrysostom: he thought that if relatives were allowed to marry they would do so without love merely to keep property in the family. Theodore Beza harps on the confusion that would ensue if relatives were allowed to marry: if, for example, a man were to marry his stepmother's mother, he would be father and son to the same person. This sort of thing would be intolerable, so that laws had very properly been enacted to prevent such marriages.

Robert Burton (1577–1640), author of the *Anatomy*

of Melancholy, can, according to Huth, claim the distinction of being the first writer to advance the theory that the marriage of relatives is forbidden because inbreeding is bad for the offspring—as we have seen, Pope Gregory I believed that there would be no offspring. In Burton's view God caused Europe to be overrun by hordes of barbarians at regular intervals in order that the evil effects of inbreeding and luxury might be remedied.

Bishop Jeremy Taylor gives several reasons for the prohibition ; that it is a contradiction of rights that any one should be at once the superior and inferior of the same person ; that there is a natural abhorrence of such mixtures ; that brothers and sisters would not have a chance of choosing elsewhere, and would marry while yet too young ; that brothers might fall in love with the same sister, and quarrel in consequence. He ridicules the projectors of the Canon Law ; some of them were for forbidding marriage to the fourth degree on the ground that there are four quarters of the world ; 'others who are graver and wiser observe 'cunningly, that besides the four humors of the body, 'there are three faculties of the Soul, which being 'joined together make seven, and they point out to 'us that men are to abstain till the seventh generation'.

Amyraut thought that there is an innate horror of incest ; it would be unnatural for a man to be subject to a woman as her son and at the same time monarch over her as her husband ; while in our sisters we see the representatives of our mother. Dugard has heard that marriages of cousins-german do not thrive, and that they are said by the Pope to be barren. He finds the common people most bitter against such marriages, which they believed brought ill luck—their horses died, their orchards 'did not hit', and their flocks were devastated by the rot. It is interesting to find the idea of incest as a national catastrophe in modern Europe. Lawrence is very much against marriages contrary to the laws of nature, whatever these may be, and instances the people of Carthagena, who 'allow not marriage with the Sister on this 'Tradition, That one who married his Sister was for 'that offence, carried and confin'd to the Moon, where 'he still remains the spot, or Man in the Moon'.

Montesquieu gives difference in age as the principal cause of marriage prohibitions; and in this he is followed by Huth himself, who winds up his investigation with these words: 'As far then as a deduction 'can be trusted from the general customs of men, no 'marriage is prohibited by nature unless the parties 'are of an age unsuited to each other'. We may contrast this dictum with that of Atkinson, whose considered opinion it is[1] that 'this form of incest '[*sc.* father-daughter] in no way creates the utter 'horror which we find universal at any union between 'brother and sister'.

---

[1] Op. cit., p. 261.

CHAPTER XIV

SUMMARY OF THEORIES

THE following is a summary of the theories which have been put forward to account for the fact that marriage between near relatives is prohibited.

Because such marriages are sterile.—Pope Gregory I.

Because the children of such marriages are weak in mind or body.—Robert Burton, L. H. Morgan, Sir E. B. Tylor.

Because there is an instinct which forbids such marriages.—St. Augustine, Professors Hobhouse and Lowie, Dr. Westermarck.

Because such marriages are unnatural.—Plato, Novatian, Amyraut, Dr. Havelock Ellis.

Because such marriages would tend to take place between persons of disproportionate age.—Socrates, Montesquieu, Huth.

As a relic of a once universal practice of marriage by capture.—J. F. MacLennan, Herbert Spencer, Lord Avebury, Mr. H. G. Wells.

Because relationship would become confused.—Theodore Beza.

Because respect for a father precludes marriage with his wife.—Philo, Agathias and Statius.

Because marriages within the family would be without love.—Luther.

Because such marriages would lead to excessive love within the family.—Aristotle, St. Chrysostom.

Because such marriages led, or would lead, to family jars of various kinds.—Bishop Jeremy Taylor, J. J. Atkinson, Professor Malinowski, Mr. Briffault, Mrs. Seligman.

From a growing regard for the domestic proprieties.—Dr. Marett.

In order to promote chastity by compelling people to seek mates at a distance.—Thomas Aquinas.

As a penance for a primeval parricide.—Freud.

Because such marriages became a royal prerogative.—Professor Elliot Smith.

For magical, religious, or superstitious reasons.—Sir J. Frazer, Professor Durkheim, A. E. Crawley, Dr. Raymond Firth.

It is of course impossible, in so small a space, to summarize accurately and completely the views of the writers cited, and the foregoing is by no means intended as a précis of the preceding chapters. Its object is to show at a glance the number and variety of the theories which have been advanced—how theologian has differed from theologian, philosopher from philosopher, and scientist from scientist. It should convince any one who, having got so far, still believes that there is some simple and obvious solution, that this is not the case.

There are, as we have seen, serious objections to all the theories which have hitherto been advanced, and quite possibly there are equally serious objections to the theory which will be advanced in this book, but I shall try to guard against what I consider to be the errors of previous writers. First I shall consider what a taboo is, and state clearly what I understand by the term; secondly, I shall survey the incest laws

SUMMARY OF THEORIES

of the world, and try to learn from them, and not from my imagination, what incest actually is ; thirdly, I shall not assume that the incest taboo exists in a state of complete independence of every other law and custom, but shall consider it in connexion with other taboos, especially those on relations between the sexes ; and fourthly, I shall consider the part which incest has played and still plays in the myth and ritual of many peoples. If I fail to solve the problem, I shall at any rate have the satisfaction of knowing that I have approached it in a scientific manner.

CHAPTER XV

MAGIC AND TABOO

IN the *Science of Life*[1] by Messrs. Wells and Huxley, we are told of 'tabu, that is primitive moral control, 'and magic, which is primitive science'. It will be the object of this chapter to show what magic and taboo are, and that there is no justification for drawing any such distinction between them. For this purpose I shall rely chiefly on Sir James Frazer, for while some of his conclusions are open to objection, it would be difficult to improve upon the completeness and lucidity with which he sets out the facts. The reader is referred to Chapters III and IV of the abridged edition of *The Golden Bough*, but argument, like legislation, by reference is unsatisfactory, and we will therefore run through those chapters, picking out such sentences as appear most pertinent to our purpose.

The principles of thought on which magic is based will be found to resolve themselves into two : first that like produces like, or that an effect resembles its cause ; and second, that things which have once been in contact with each other continue to act on each other at a distance after the physical contact has been severed. Charms based on the first may be called Homœopathic or Imitative Magic ; those based on the second may be called Contagious Magic. The magician tacitly assumes that the Laws of Similarity and Contact are of universal application ; magic, in short, is a spurious system of natural law as well as

[1] p. 868.

a fallacious guide of conduct ; it is a false science as well as an abortive art. At the same time it must be borne in mind that the primitive magician knows magic only on its practical side ; he never analyses the mental processes on which is practice his based, never reflects on the abstract principles involved in his actions. With him, as with the vast majority of men, logic is implicit, not explicit ; to him magic is always an art, never a science : the very idea of science is lacking in his undeveloped mind.

Perhaps the most familiar example of Homœopathic Magic is the attempt which has been made by many people in many ages to injure or destroy an enemy by injuring or destroying an image of him, in the belief that, just as the image suffers, so does the man, and that when it perishes he must die. Thousands of years ago the practice was known to the sorcerers of ancient India, Babylon, and Egypt, as well as of Greece and Rome, and at this day it is still resorted to by cunning and malignant savages in Australia, Africa, and Scotland, and among the North American Indians and the Malays.

A curious application of the doctrine of Contagious Magic is the relation commonly believed to exist between the wounded man and the agent of the wound, so that whatever is subsequently done by or to the agent must correspondingly affect the patient either for good or evil. Thus Pliny tells us that if you have wounded a man and are sorry for it, you have only to spit on the hand that gave the wound, and the pains of the sufferer will be instantly alleviated. In Melanesia, if a man's friends get possession of the arrow that wounded him, they keep it in a damp place, for then the inflammation will soon subside. ' It is constantly received and avouched ', says Bacon, ' that the anointing of the weapon that maketh the ' wound will heal the wound itself', and he goes on to give the recipe for such ointment, which includes ' the moss upon the skull of a dead man unburied '. Remedies of the sort which Bacon deemed worthy of his attention are still in vogue in the eastern counties of England. Thus in Suffolk if a man cuts himself with a billhook or a scythe, he always takes care to keep the weapon bright, and oils it to prevent the wound from festering. Similarly, Cambridgeshire labourers think that if a horse has run a nail into its foot it is necessary to grease the nail and put it away in some safe place, or the horse will not recover. Superstitions of the same character are widespread in Germany, and are reported from America and Central Australia.

But it is to be observed that the system of magic is not merely composed of positive precepts ; it comprises a very large number of negative precepts, that is, prohibitions. The positive precepts are charms ; the negative precepts are taboos. Positive magic or sorcery says, ' Do this in order that so-and-so may ' happen '. Negative magic or taboo says, ' Do not ' do this lest so-and-so should happen '. Both consequences, the desirable and the undesirable, are supposed to be brought about in accordance with the laws of similarity and contact. And just as the desired consequence is not really effected by the observance of a magical ceremony, so the dreaded consequence does not really result from the violation of a taboo. Those negative precepts which we call taboo are just as futile as those positive precepts which we call sorcery. The two things are merely opposite sides or poles of one great and disastrous fallacy.

When we survey the races of mankind we observe that they are distinguished from one another by a great variety of religions; yet when we have penetrated through these differences, which affect mainly the intelligent and thoughtful part of the community, we shall find underlying them all a solid stratum of intellectual agreement among the dull, the weak, the ignorant, and the superstitious, who constitute, unfortunately, the vast majority of mankind. This universal faith, this truly Catholic creed, is a belief in the efficacy of magic. If the test of truth lay in a show of hands or a counting of heads, the system of magic might appeal, with far more reason than the Catholic Church, to the proud motto, *Quod semper, quod ubique, quod ab omnibus*, as the sure and certain credential of its own infallibility.

In the foregoing, the words are those of Sir James, with the exception of some slight alterations made for the purposes of abridgment. Far from exaggerating the universality of magic, he has in fact underestimated it, since he confines its influence to the dull and ignorant. The following is a selection from the long list of magical rites and taboos which are generally performed or observed by the educated and intelligent inhabitants of Britain:

Magical Rites and Practices

To wear a 'lucky' coin on the watch-chain.
To carry a mascot on the car.
To wear a ring to guard against rheumatism.

To turn the coins in one's pocket when one sees the new moon.

To walk round one's chair to change one's luck at cards.

Taboos

To tell a dream before breakfast.

To break a mirror.

To see the new moon through glass.

To reverse a garment which has been accidentally put on inside out.

To cut the nails on Sunday.

To start a journey on Friday, or on the thirteenth of the month.

To cross knives.

To give or receive a knife as a present.

To wear a green tie.

To spill the salt.

To allow a glass to ring out.

To proceed along a road which a magpie has crossed.

To light three cigarettes from one match.

To congratulate oneself on one's luck.

To sit down thirteen at table.

To some of these taboos there are recognized magical antidotes :—

It is safe to proceed along a road which a magpie has crossed, if one salutes the magpie.

It is safe to congratulate oneself on one's luck, if at the same time one 'touches wood' (and says 'Unberufen !').

No harm comes of spilling the salt, if one throws three pinches over one's left shoulder.

The existence of these magical antidotes shows

clearly that taboo is nothing but negative magic, and has no connection with morality.

It is worth while pausing for a moment to consider the taboo against sitting down thirteen at table, which is interesting since it preserves the primitive idea of breach of taboo as dangerous to the community; for it is not believed that it is the person who sits down last, and who might be supposed to be an object of especial resentment to the powers that be, who is destined for an early death, but that the lot may fall on any member of the company. It is unquestionably a taboo, and a social taboo at that, so that if we credit Freud, who tells us[1] that 'the basis 'of taboo is a forbidden action for which there exists 'a strong inclination in the unconscious', and Professor Malinowski, who assures us[2] that 'a social 'taboo does not derive its force from instinct, but 'that instead it always has to work against some 'innate impulse', we must suppose that England is full of people suffering from a neurosis as a consequence of suppressing their innate impulse to sit down thirteen at table. Whatever the origin of this taboo, nobody seriously supposes it to be either instinctive or natural, or to be of any moral, material, or social benefit to the community, and what applies to this taboo applies to most others.

How do taboos arise? We can see them arising daily. A man has a couple of accidents when driving along a particular road; he says that the road is unlucky, and vows never to drive along it again. In other words, he supposes that the *genius loci* is hostile to him, and therefore places himself under a taboo. About a century ago, in England, a man was buried

---

[1] Op. cit., p. 54. [2] Op. cit., p. 199.

under a stone upon which he had had inscribed a curse upon any one who should move it. Last year, so I read in a newspaper, this stone was found to be in the way of a road improvement, but the county council was afraid to touch it; a taboo had been established. This is how taboos arise now, and this is how, in the absence of evidence to the contrary, we must suppose that they have always arisen. The idea that any taboo was ever instituted with the rational object of conferring some benefit on humanity is contrary to both reason and experience.

The examples of magic and taboo given above, which could easily be added to,[1] are those in force among the 'educated' of both sexes, but women have in addition a large number to themselves; a whole volume could be written on the magical rites and taboos observed by the 'educated' bride, and her child is usually born into a room in which there is a great deal more magic than fresh air.

Besides all these amateur efforts, the British people still maintains a large number of professional magicians — astrologers, crystal-gazers, palmists, and fortune-tellers by cards; diviners and dowsers; exorcists, mediums, and necromancers; makers and sellers of amulets, charms, and mascots. It is, however, amusing to note that the only people who still call themselves magicians are the members of that least superstitious of bodies, the Magic Circle.

Many living creatures, such as cats, hares, owls, swallows, spiders, have magical associations, as well as many plants and jewels, and the prevalence of

---

[1] For an admirable study of American student magic see *Social Origins and Social Continuities* by Prof. A. M. Tozzer, of Harvard.

magical ideas is illustrated by the common use of the words ' lucky ' and ' unlucky ', and of such phrases as ' it worked like magic ' ; ' He bore a charmed life ' ; ' I did it in an evil hour '.

Many of the examples which I have given may seem trivial, and taken individually so no doubt they are, but collectively they are important as showing the immense influence which magic has among all classes in the most civilized countries. But great as is the influence of magic in England to-day, we have ample evidence that two or three centuries ago it was very much greater still, and that among all savages it is even greater, occupying not only the position which it occupies among ourselves, but also those which are here occupied by religion and science.

We know also that many of our most valuable institutions and cherished customs were of magical origin ; singing and poetry were originally used for incantations, writing for spells ; our dances are compounded of round dances, intended to promote the proper functioning of the heavenly bodies, of war-dances intended to secure victory, and of jumping dances intended to induce the crops to grow high ; and so on with the drama, with ball-games, and many others. On the other hand, we know of no old custom or institution of which we can say that it originated in instinct or in reason. These being the facts, for facts they are, it might be supposed that any writer putting forward a non-magical theory of the origin of some old institution, such as exogamy, would feel bound to state clearly his reasons for rejecting a magical origin ; but so far is this from being the case, that one may search through whole libraries of books on philosophy, history, sociology, psychology, and ethics without finding any reference to magic at all.

The explanation of the astonishing fact that in any discussion of human origins the most universal and powerful motive force in human conduct, a force which seems to lie behind all the institutions, customs, and beliefs of savages, even those which seem to us to be rational, and consequently behind that very large proportion of our own institutions, customs, and beliefs which are derived from savagery, is almost invariably ignored, is not easy to find, but is probably to be sought in the classical tradition. The ancient Greek philosophers were logicians rather than scientists; they were interested in a theoretical future rather than in the actual past, and their discussions took the form of attempts to test the logical consistency of highly theoretical speculations rather than of attempts to ascertain, compare, and interpret facts. To postulate a magical origin for any Greek custom would have been dull, since it would afford no basis for speculation, and degrading, since it was not to be supposed that a philosopher could be influenced by mere superstition. With their minds working on these lines they inevitably came to the conclusion that everything that was done or thought must have an adequate basis in nature or in reason, and they had no difficulty in inventing such bases when necessary.

When the study of philosophy was revived at the Renaissance the mental attitude of the Greek philosophers was revived with it, and has persisted till the present day. The path which Montaigne pointed out was not followed, and it was, and still is, considered both unnecessary and undignified for a philosopher to illustrate his theories by the facts of everyday life. Thus it is that Professor Hobhouse was able to write his *Morals in Evolution* without a single reference to magic, and that Professor McDougall is prepared to postulate an infinite variety of instincts rather than admit the possibility that magic has ever influenced the conduct of any human being.

Sir James Frazer broke away from this tradition, and his writings have had great influence, but much less than they might have had, had he not adopted and adhered to the belief, which was general when he first wrote, that the same ideas and practices, the same tools and weapons, are found in different parts of the world because the human mind invariably and inevitably works along the same lines. This doctrine of the independent creation of custom is just as fatal to the study of sociology as was the doctrine of the independent creation of species to the study of biology; in both cases you name your species and catalogue your specimens, and you have come to the end of your science. The result is that Sir James has few actual disciples, and that the social anthropologists of to-day are divided into two schools—the functionalists who, continuing in the ancient Greek tradition, endeavour to explain all human conduct rationally, and the diffusionists. A chapter will be devoted to the latter, and here it need only be said that their theories permit magic to take its place as the most powerful influence upon human conduct that the world has yet seen.

I will conclude by stating that if, as I believe, the incest taboo is really a taboo, then it is a magical prohibition, and that if it is not a magical prohibition, then it is not a taboo.

CHAPTER XVI

WHAT IS INCEST?

WE have seen that Atkinson, Crawley, Frazer, Professor Elliot Smith, and Dr. Havelock Ellis would derive the incest taboo from a prohibition of intercourse between brother and sister, and Mr. Briffault agrees with them.[1] On the other hand, Huth, Freud, Mrs. Seligman, and G. A. Dorsey[2] would base it on the parent child relationship; and with them is Professor Malinowski, who says[3] that if it were not for the incest taboo 'the normal relation of 'the child to the father and mother would be destroyed'. Several of these writers account very plausibly for the particular type of incest taboo which they suppose to be the original one, but they fail completely when they attempt to explain how this type led to the other type, and none of them even attempts to explain how either of these types led, for example, to the taboo on marriage with a deceased wife's sister.

It seems to me that the first step towards ascertaining how the incest taboo arose is to ascertain what it actually is, and with this end in view I shall first consider the word 'incest', and then shall make a brief survey first of the incest laws of civilized peoples and then of savages; by so doing I hope to ensure that any theories which I shall formulate shall have an adequate foundation in fact.

The word 'incest' is derived from the Latin, but the Romans had no word for incest; *incestus*, originally

---

[1] Mothers, I, p. 257.   [2] *Civilization*, p. 92.   [3] Op. cit., p. 252.

WHAT IS INCEST?

'ritually impure', was applied to prohibited marriages, but also to many other offences and improprieties. We find a similar phenomenon in Arabic; a prohibited marriage is *bâtil*, 'spurious', and so is a bad penny. There appears to be no word for incest in any savage language.[1] Reserving comment on these facts, we will now consider what the word 'incest' is alleged to mean. Dr. Johnson defined it as 'unnatural and 'criminal conjunction of persons within degrees 'prohibited', which suggests that nature is regulated by Act of Parliament. Modern lexicographers avoid the word 'unnatural'. Skeat gives simply 'unchastity,' while Chambers gives 'sexual intercourse within the 'prohibited degrees of kindred'. A number of others have 'the crime of cohabitation or sexual commerce 'between persons related within the degrees wherein 'marriage is prohibited by law' (Webster), or words to the same effect. The *New English Dictionary* has in addition 'sexual commerce of near kindred'; but none of them admits the possibility of an incestuous marriage, or realizes that incest can be of more than one type.

As a fact, what is regarded as incest in this country is of three distinct types—that which is criminal, such as intercourse with a daughter; that which is illegal but not criminal, such as marriage with a niece; and that which is sinful but not illegal, such as marriage with a deceased wife's sister. This state of affairs is transitional, and it is transitional in the direction of removing restrictions on marriage, a process the exact opposite of that postulated by the theorists, who suppose all incest laws to be extensions of simple prohibitions either of brother-sister or of parent-child incest.

[1] But see note p. 197.

To continue our survey—the Church of England regards as incestuous several types of marriage which are now valid by the law of England, while the latter would regard as incestuous, though not criminally so, a marriage which a Roman Catholic would be bound to regard as valid, that is to say, a marriage between uncle and niece which had been sanctioned by the Pope. It does not appear that a Pope has recently sanctioned such a marriage, but up to the eighteenth century he often did so. It is doubtful whether there are two countries in Europe in which the incest laws are exactly the same, and such differences are no new phenomenon, since these questions were long in dispute among theologians, in whose discretion the matter formerly rested. The Churches have ceased to insist that the marriage of those who are godparents to the same child is as incestuous as that of brother and sister; it appears that this view, formerly universal throughout Christendom, now only survives in corners of the Balkans.

The incest laws of Islam[1] prohibit the marriage of persons nearly connected by kindred and affinity, and forbid a man to marry two nearly related women at the same time. They have also two types of incest unknown among Christians—marriage or intercourse between relations by fosterage, and marriage between fellow-pilgrims. Among the Shiahs marriage is forbidden for fosterage in the same order as in the case of consanguinity; the Sunnis make some exceptions. ' The relationship of fosterage arises among the Shiahs ' when the child has been really nourished at the breast ' of the foster-mother. Among the Sunnis it is required

[1] T. P. Hughes, *Dictionary of Islam*, p. 317.

'that the child should have been suckled at least 'fifteen times, or at least a day and a night. Among 'the Hanafis it is enough if it has been suckled only 'once. Among the Shafais it is necessary that it 'should have been suckled four times'. It will be seen that the line dividing a valid from an incestuous marriage is a very fine one. The laws regarding marriage between fellow-pilgrims are similarly complex; by most sects they are regarded as illegal, in some cases imposing a taboo on the parties for life. I find it impossible to believe that these regulations, whose complexity is only equalled by their absurdity, are derived from one or two simple laws, deliberately imposed upon themselves by a group of rationally-minded savages.

The Jewish laws have tended, like those of Christianity, which they may have copied, to bar marriages which the Mosaic code permitted, such as those between uncle and niece, but otherwise call for no mention here; and of the classical incest laws we need only mention that the Greeks allowed marriage with a half-sister on the father's but not on the mother's side, while the chief difference between Romans and Christians was that among the former kinship by adoption was, as it now is among the Hindus, equivalent to blood-relationship.

Among the Chinese persons with the same surname are forbidden to marry, even if they come from opposite ends of the empire; and similarly we are told that among certain Californian tribes the marriage of accidental namesakes is forbidden.[1]

The foregoing could of course be greatly extended,

[1] A. L. Kroeber, *Tribes of California*, p. 493.

but my object has been, while I hope omitting no important point, merely to mention such facts as must necessarily be taken into account in attempting to put forward a satisfactory solution of the problem. These facts make it clear, even before we have considered the incest laws of savages, that none of the proposed definitions of incest will do, and it is difficult to find a better definition than that incest is marriage or sexual intercourse which is prohibited on the ground that there is some other connexion between the parties.

When we examine the kinship and marriage laws of the more primitive races, we find that they are strikingly different from our own. Among the most widespread laws or customs are :

(1) Exogamy, which means that a tribe is divided into two or more groups, usually totemic clans, and that members of the same group may not marry, even when there is no traceable relationship between them.

(2) Cross-cousin marriage, which means that a man's proper wife is the daughter of his mother's brother or father's sister, or a girl who is both.

(3) Fraternal polyandry, which usually means that younger brothers have a right of access to the wife or wives of the eldest brother.

(4) Sororal polygyny, which usually means that a man has the right to marry his wife's sisters.

(5) Matrilineal descent, which means that both sexes derive their membership of the group, clan, or totem from their mother, and not from their father ; with this often goes the system by which all property descends in the female line.

WHAT IS INCEST?

(6) Matrilocal marriage, which means that a woman continues to live with her mother after her marriage, and that her husband either comes to live with her, or merely visits her from time to time.

It would be difficult, perhaps impossible, to find a tribe in which all these laws or customs are still observed, and there are of course many tribes whose usages, in some at least of these respects, more closely resemble our own, but the distribution of these customs at the present day, and the traces of them which appear to survive among peoples which do not now observe them, suggest that quite possibly they represent the pattern upon which early society was organized, and that the patriarchal family is as much out of place in the primeval forest as its Victorian ally the top-hat.

Exogamy is so widespread among savages that I do not propose to trace its distribution, but cross-cousin marriage is equally germane to our problem, and its distribution presents some interesting features. As we have seen, the cross-cousin whom a man marries may be his mother's brother's daughter, his father's sister's daughter, or a girl who is both; in some cases marriage with only one type is permitted, and while marriage with the proper cross-cousin is sometimes compulsory, many cases occur in which alternative matches, with a second cousin, niece, or other relative, are permitted. It would take a good deal of space, and seems unnecessary, to distinguish what are merely varieties of the same custom.

Let us begin with Asia. Among the Hindus[1] the

[1] These examples, unless otherwise stated, are from FOT, II, pp. 98-193.

marriage of first cousins is strictly prohibited, and cross-cousin marriage is therefore rare in Northern India, but it is general in Central India, and in Southern India is practically universal, even among the Brahmans. It is here that marriage with a sister's daughter, who since descent is patrilineal does not belong to the same clan, is a frequent alternative. In Ceylon cross-cousin marriage is universal, and it is almost universal in Assam and Burma. In Tibet it is forbidden, and it is very rare in China, but common in Siberia. In the East Indies the practice varies; while forbidden in Java it is common in Sumatra, and the rule in Timor. Matters are much the same in Melanesia; while cross-cousin marriage is the rule in Fiji, New Caledonia, and the New Hebrides, it is forbidden in New Ireland, the Banks Islands, and most of New Guinea. In Polynesia it is forbidden, while in Australia it is the rule in about half of the tribes, and strictly forbidden in the other half, though in some of the latter tribes the children of cross-cousins are the proper match. Crossing to America we find that it is there the exception rather than the rule, but it occurs among a number of North American tribes and is reported among the Caribs, and some tribes of Guiana and Brazil. In Africa its distribution is also sporadic; it is the rule among the Ashanti in the west, the Bechuana in the south, and a number of other tribes; but in many cases it is stringently prohibited, and in Uganda was punishable with death.

We thus find, in most parts of the world, areas in which cross-cousin marriage is the rule adjacent to areas in which it is regarded as incestuous. To give two particular examples—in Central Australia two kinship systems, the Kariera and the Dieri, are followed by tribes at the same very low level of culture; with the former cross-cousin marriage is the rule, while with the latter it is forbidden.[1] Similarly, in Rhodesia we find two adjacent tribes, the Awemba and the Winamwanga; the former marry their cross-cousins, but regard with horror the idea of marrying their father's widows, while the customs of the latter are the exact opposite.[2]

These instances show clearly the absurdity of assuming that this, or any other, custom necessarily arose in the area in which we now find it, or was based on the needs and local conditions of the peoples which now practise it. How it arose we shall consider later.

We must now note the existence of the opposite custom to cross-cousin marriage, that is, ortho-cousin marriage; this may take two forms, marriage with the father's brother's daughter and marriage with the mother's sister's daughter. The latter seems, if not unknown, to be extremely rare, while the former, though widespread, is almost peculiar to Moslems. It is, and has been from time immemorial, the rule in Arabia, and, though no part of the Moslem religion, has been carried by its missionaries as far as Nigeria on the west and at least as far as India on the east. This shows how, in favourable circumstances, a custom can be adopted by people who have previously held the idea of it in abhorrence, and further shows the absurdity of assuming that customs are indigenous and locally conditioned. Generally speaking, this practice is in extreme disfavour among savages, and

[1] A. P. Elkin, in *Oceania*, Vol. II, pp. 54 seq.
[2] FOT, II, pp. 153-5.

we must suppose that some special cause must have operated to bring it into favour with the Arabs and ancient Greeks, the only peoples which appear to have made it the rule in pre-Islamic times. What this special cause was we must try to ascertain.

Frazer points out the general favour shown by savages to cross-cousin marriage and the general hostility to ortho-cousin marriage, and concludes that they are the result of the dual organization, of which I shall have more to say later, though I may mention here that it involves the division of a community into two exogamous halves. He supposes that the dual organization was deliberately instituted to prevent incest, from which view I have already dissented. Professor Durkheim and Mr. Briffault have supposed that the dual organization arose as a result of marriage alliances between pairs of clans, but there seems no reason to believe that the clan was ever anything but a section of a tribe, and the theory, apart from other considerations, necessitates the attribution to our ancestors of powers of organized diplomacy at an impossibly early date. Mr. Briffault says [1]: 'The 'primary motive which leads the Australian aborigines, 'the Melanesians, or the people of Upper Burma to 'provide for intermarriage with a group different from 'their own, and the first and foremost consideration 'which governs all their marriage regulations, is the 'dread of incest and the desire to avoid it by every 'possible means. But, paradoxically as it may appear, 'the very means adopted to avoid marrying a person 'belonging to their own group and related to them, leads 'them to marry persons who are, we should consider,

[1] Mothers, I, p. 587.

WHAT IS INCEST?

'closely related to them.' And who are in fact closely related to them! It would indeed be a paradox if, as Mr. Briffault and other writers suppose, all these races compelled near relatives to marry with the sole object of preventing near relatives from marrying, but there is no good reason for believing that they do anything of the kind. When we find people who marry their nieces as a matter of duty, while they regard with horror the idea of marriage with women who are not related to them at all, it is, or should be, sufficiently obvious that their horror of incest is not based on a horror of marriage between relatives. We have seen that there is no justification for believing that the laws of savages are deliberately intended to prevent anything, but what their marriage laws actually do prevent is a breach of the rule of group exogamy. Incest is not, among the more primitive races, a substantive offence, but is merely a breach of the law, which provides that no man may have intercourse, except on certain ritual occasions to which we shall refer later, with a woman of his own group, whether she be a relative or not.

The marriage codes of the world may be divided into two types—Type I, which includes the great majority of savages, in which all marriage within the exogamous group, which is that of one parent, is forbidden, but instead of marriage outside the group being freely permitted there are usually modifications barring marriage with the other parent and perhaps with some of his or her relatives. Type II, which includes Christians, Jews and Moslems, and some savages, in which there is no exogamous group, but marriage with relatives on both sides is prohibited in an equal but varying degree, and a new feature, prohibition of marriage with the wife's or husband's relatives (apart from the mother-in-law, whom we shall consider separately) is introduced.

The Chinese and orthodox Hindus are more or less intermediate, the former inclining towards Type I and the latter towards Type II. The existence of these two types is totally inconsistent with the view that incest began with the prohibition of intercourse between parent and child or brother and sister, but is consistent with the view that a particular modification differentiated Type II from Type I, and that the same modification in a simpler form differentiated Type I from simple exogamy. We must conclude that no incest law could have arisen till group exogamy was established, and that the original incest law was simply a taboo on the breach of group exogamy. How this taboo arose, and what was the modification which led to all the differences, complications, inconsistencies, and anomalies which we find in the incest laws of the world, we must now try to ascertain.

CHAPTER XVII

WHY IS A MENSTRUOUS WOMAN TABOO?

ONE of the principal reasons why those who have theorized on the incest taboo have failed really to get to grips with the subject is that they have regarded it an an isolated phenomenon, instead of considering it in connexion with other taboos on relations between the sexes. There is one taboo which appears to share with the incest taboo the distinction of being universal, and that is the taboo on menstruous women. Not only have these two taboos had a vast influence on the conduct of mankind in general, but it would be hardly an exaggeration to say that they have between them conditioned the sexual life of women in all ages and in all countries; one of them tells a woman when she may have intercourse and the other with whom she may have intercourse. As soon as this fact is realized, the idea presents itself that the two taboos are connected, and that either they are derived from a common source, or one is derived from the other.

The various forms which the taboo on menstruous women may take can be divided into three classes:

(1) She must avoid all connexion with men.
(2) She must avoid all connexion with other people's food or cooking utensils.
(3) She must avoid water, especially running water.

To give some examples of the first; throughout North America menstruous women were secluded.

Among many tribes a menstruous woman must take elaborate precautions to avoid touching any tool or weapon belonging to a man, and to ensure that no man follows her unwittingly along a path, for it is believed that if a man were to tread in the track of a menstruous woman he would have sore legs. A similar belief is held by the tribes of the Orinoco, and throughout South as well as North America the most rigorous precautions are taken to avoid dangers from menstruous women, and especially girls at their first menstruation. In many cases they have to fast for long periods in special huts far from the men, and even then the Delawares do not feel safe, so a girl's eyes are bandaged for twelve days, lest she should happen to see any one. In Brazil girls are sewn up into a hammock, which is hung over a fire, and they are starved and fumigated for several days, not seldom with fatal results. Among the tribes of Siberia menstruous women must not touch anything which is used by men. According to the Mosaic law anything that a menstruous woman had sat or lain upon was unclean, and any one who touched it had to undergo ritual purification. Similarly, the Hindu law declared that a menstruous woman who touched a man should be whipped. The wild tribes of Bengal believe that the greatest misfortunes would befall any one who looked upon a menstruous woman. Throughout South and West Africa menstruous women are, among nearly all the tribes, completely segregated, and similar rules obtain in the East Indies, the Pacific Islands, and Australia. An Australian black who found that his wife had used his blanket during her period killed her and died of fright. In New Guinea it is believed that a man who saw a menstruous woman

WHY IS A MENSTRUOUS WOMAN TABOO?

would swell up and die; the Déné Indians believe that contact with menstrual blood will turn a man into a woman, while some South African tribes believe that the touch of a menstruous woman will cause a man's bones to become soft.

Having given some examples of the appalling results which are believed to follow from contact, however slight or accidental, between a man and a menstruous woman, we next come to the food taboo. In America the usage varies to some extent; among some tribes a menstruating woman may not even touch her own food, but is fed by another woman; among others she may cook for herself, but the vessels she has used are broken immediately afterwards. In Persia a menstruous woman's food had to be cooked separately, and she received it with her hand wrapped in a cloth. Among the Hindus of the Punjab a girl at her first menstruation must not consume milk, oil, or meat. The Nayar women of Madras had to be fed by other women out of special vessels. Among the Baila of Rhodesia a menstruous woman is not segregated, as she is among many South African tribes, but she must not cook her husband's food. In Ceram, in the East Indies, a young woman was executed not many years ago for eating a fish during her period. In the Gilbert Islands coco-nuts on trees growing within a hundred feet of the dwelling of a menstruous woman are considered unfit for human consumption. The Romans believed that growing corn withered and wine turned sour at the approach of a menstruous woman.[1]

In many parts of the world women are, as we have

---

[1] The foregoing examples are from R. Briffault, *The Mothers*, II, pp. 365 seq.

seen, shut up or secluded at their periods, and the water taboo is only evident where they are freer. Frazer tells us [1] that in the Greek island of Calymnos a menstruous woman must not draw water from a well, or cross a running stream. Captain Rattray gives several examples from Ashanti ; he tells us [2] that the water for the Adae ceremony must be drawn by a woman who has passed the menopause ; that the Apo ceremony is performed at night, when there is no risk of the water having been polluted by a menstruous woman [3], and that no menstruous woman may cross the River Tano ; if her menses come on when she is on a visit to the other side, she must stay there.[4] Similarly, in Australia menstruous women must not approach the Murray River ; they would scare the fish.[5]

In parts of Bohemia and Moravia a woman crossing a bridge for the first time after childbirth drops some money into the water.[6] Taboos on women before and immediately after childbirth are often similar to those on menstruous women.

The Akamba of East Africa believe that married women can only conceive during their periods, and intercourse is therefore the rule at those times ; but unmarried girls must be careful to avoid both intercourse and water-carrying when menstruous.[7]

Vestiges of all three forms of the taboo still survive in England. Not only must a menstruous woman avoid sexual intercourse, but it is still widely believed that she cannot cure bacon and that she should not bathe ; Mr. Warren R. Dawson tells me of a Kentish

---

[1] GB, X, p. 97. [2] *Ashanti*, p. 95. [3] Ibid., p. 165. [4] Ibid., p. 202.
[5] Brough Smith, *Aborigines of Victoria*, I, p. 236.
[6] Frazer, *The Fasti of Ovid*, IV, p. 97.
[7] G. Lindblom, *The Akamba*, p. 39.

WHY IS A MENSTRUOUS WOMAN TABOO? 113

maidservant who during her period refused to enter the bathroom to turn on her mistress's bath.

The theories which have been put forward to account for this taboo follow the usual course; the survival most prominent in this country, the taboo on sexual intercourse, is assumed to be the original form of the taboo, and explanations are invented which might account for that form, but fail completely to account for the other forms which the taboo assumes. Thus it has been suggested that women in their periods have an instinctive distaste for intercourse, and that the taboo was ordained to protect them, at those times, from the unwelcome attentions of the men. We have already seen that taboos are not ordained for specific purposes; but apart from this it is to be objected in the first place, that since civilized nations have not thought it necessary to protect women from mad, drunken, or diseased husbands it is unlikely that savages would be more squeamish, and in the second place that it is quite untrue that menstruous women have a distaste for sexual intercourse. Dr. Havelock Ellis tells us [1] that 'on the psychic side the chief normal 'and primitive characteristic of the menstrual state 'is the more predominant presence of the sexual 'impulse', and goes on to say that this fact is often concealed by extraneous causes; we may safely say that the principal extraneous causes are superstitions such as the belief, general among Englishwomen of all classes, that birthmarks are due to conception during menstruation.

An alternative theory is that men who have intercourse with menstruous women suffer from some form

[1] *Studies*, I, p. 100.

of disease; this is pure imagination, but in any case it is impossible to suppose that laws enacted to protect women against men or men against women could induce a belief that menstruous women cannot cure bacon.

Mr. Briffault [1] gives many examples of the belief that menstruation is caused by the moon, and if it were merely a question of sexual intercourse we might suppose that it is fear of the moon which induces the savage to avoid menstruous women; as we have seen, however, the taboo goes much further than that, and as the taboos imposed on parturient women are often the same as, or similar to, those imposed on menstruous women, we are forced to conclude that what the savage fears is not the moon, but something that emanates from the woman herself, and especially her blood.

Dr. Marett, as we have seen, speaks of ' the mothers, 'whose blood was the symbol of social decency and ' honour '; whatever we understand by ' symbol ', whether emblem, substitute, or representation, we cannot envisage menstrual blood as a symbol of decency and honour, and the reader can judge for himself how much of decency and honour there is in the customs and beliefs which we have just summarized.

Professor Durkheim supposed, as we saw, that human blood, however shed, had to be revenged, but it does not appear that this is the correct solution. Animal blood is greatly used by savages, both for food and in ritual, and human blood is used similarly in cannibal feasts, and rites of initiation and brotherhood; generally speaking no horror is attached, and where there is such horror it may well be transferred from menstrual

[1] Mothers, II, pp. 583 seq.

WHY IS A MENSTRUOUS WOMAN TABOO?

blood and not vice versa. Savages seem generally to regard menstrual blood very much as we do strychnine, that is to say, as a drug which is extremely dangerous if the proper precautions are not observed, but which may with such precautions be used to kill vermin or as a stimulant. By the peasants of Italy and the Indians of North America menstruous women are employed to run naked round the cornfields and thus destroy caterpillars and other pests, and among some tribes which hold menstruous women in the greatest horror a piece of rag dipped in menstrual blood is hung round the neck of ailing children.[1]

Three facts appear to emerge from the foregoing; the first is that the taboo on menstruous women is a genuine taboo, that is to say, a magical prohibition; secondly that the menstrual blood is the central feature of the taboo; and thirdly that the taboo had originally no connexion with sexual intercourse. We may perhaps suppose that the mysterious and apparently causeless character of the flow filled early man with a surprise which developed gradually into alarm, and later into horror, and that he developed *pari passu* a most elaborate system of precautions against the magical dangers which he believed to threaten him. It is possible that one of these precautions was the system of group exogamy.

---

[1] Mothers, II, p. 410.

CHAPTER XVIII

WHY MUST A MAN AVOID HIS MOTHER-IN-LAW?

ONE of the most widespread rules of savage society is that which ordains that a man shall on no account speak to, or even look upon, his mother-in-law. A few examples of this well-known rule should suffice ; in Australia, among the northern tribes, a man is warned of the approach of his mother-in-law by the sound of a bull-roarer, and a native is said to have nearly died of fright because the shadow of his mother-in-law fell on his legs while he lay asleep. In the south-east it was formerly death for a man to speak to his mother-in-law. In New Britain ' what ' calamities would result from a man's accidentally ' speaking to his mother-in-law, no native imagination ' has yet been found equal to conceiving.[1] Suicide of ' one or both would probably be the only course '. At a mission school in New Guinea a boy of six suddenly fell to the floor like a log ; he had seen his brother's mother-in-law pass the window. In Africa things are much the same ; a young Herero was attending a meeting when his fiancée's mother suddenly appeared ; he fell flat on his face and his friends piled rugs and skins on him till he was nearly suffocated. The Indians of Yucatan believe that if a man were to meet his mother-in-law he could never beget children. An Apache, meeting his mother-in-law on a rocky path, hung over a precipice, in danger of death, till she had

[1] I have amended the grammar of this sentence.

passed. Similar practices are found in many parts of the world, and the time-honoured mother-in-law joke is probably a relic of their former existence in this country.

There are three variants of this rule: the first is the avoidance by a man of all his wife's relatives; this occurs in Central Australia, for example, but is comparatively rare. The second is where a woman has to avoid her son-in-law; this is also comparatively rare, but occurs among the Pangwe of West Africa and the Modoc Indians of California; it is stated that a Modoc has the right to kill his mother-in-law if he meets her. The third is the avoidance by a woman of her father-in-law; this is very rare among savages, but is found among the more civilized and strongly patriarchal Chinese and Hindus.

Various theories have been proposed to account for this taboo; that generally accepted is that it is intended to prevent incest, but the objections to such a view seem to me to be insuperable. We have seen that savages never legislate, and that therefore it is impossible that any savage law could have been deliberately designed to achieve the object which it actually does achieve, let alone an ulterior one. To make it a capital offence for a man to place himself in a position in which he might possibly be tempted to commit an offence would be totally opposed to civilized ideas of justice; to a savage such an idea could not possibly occur. None but the most superficial observer supposes that our own rules of propriety, such as that which regulates the amount of bosom which a lady should display in evening dress, were designed to prevent improper sexual relations, but the theory invites us to suppose either that the mother-in-law taboo is unique, or that other customs and taboos were similarly designed to prevent us from being led into temptation. Do our theorists suppose that we remove our hat when we meet a lady in case she might be tempted to snatch it and make off, and that we must not bring it into the drawing-room because we might be tempted to throw it at the clock on the chimneypiece, and, if not, how, when, where, and why do they draw the line?

The fact is that taboos are magical prohibitions, and not police regulations; but apart from these general considerations the fact that the mother-in-law taboo is not intended to prevent incest appears clearly from the actual character of these taboos. Incest with a sister is everywhere considered more serious than incest with a mother-in-law, and is no doubt more tempting, since savage mothers-in-law have usually passed the period at which their charms were calculated to arouse desire in the opposite sex; yet while the mother-in-law taboo is almost universal, brother-sister avoidance, which we shall discuss later, is much less widely distributed.

Among the Akamba a man may associate freely with his mother-in-law if he presents her with an ox, and the same custom, with a horse substituted for the ox, obtains among the Arapahos of Nevada. The Navahoes, Cherokees, and other tribes of North America, and the Caribs of the West Indies, had to avoid their mothers-in-law most carefully; but if the latter happened to be widows, they could go through a form of marriage with them before marrying their daughters, and then avoidance was no longer necessary. Similarly, the Wagogo and Wahehe of East Africa have

intercourse ritually with their future mothers-in-law before marrying the daughters, and then need not avoid them. It is impossible to believe that these customs have any connexion with the prevention of incest, but the matter does not end there, for we actually find cases in which breach of the mother-in-law taboo is regarded as a more serious offence than incest:
'It is stated of the Baganda, and the remark would
'appear to be generally applicable, that they attach
'a greater degree of sanctity to the prohibition referring
'to the mother-in-law than to the prohibition against
'incest.'[1]

Dr. Westermarck's view [2] that mother-in-law avoidance is due to 'sexual modesty in the domestic circle' can hardly be taken seriously, and I cannot find that the Freudians have discovered such an urge in the subconscious. Mr. Briffault's view is [3] that 'the awe
'with which the primitive human mother was regarded,
'and her natural supremacy in the group of which she
'was the creator, have passed away before the rule
'and power of the male . . . but a memory of the
'character with which she was invested and of the
'feelings which she inspired survives in the seemingly
'absurd sentiments which everywhere among savage
'races attach to the wife's mother'. I have no doubt that Mr. Briffault is right when he says that the supposed danger comes from the mother-in-law and not from the son-in-law,[4] but to abolish the authority of the mother and then transfer it to the mother-in-law seems a difficult feat, and he fails to realize that people's fears are based not on what may have happened to

---

[1] Mothers, I, p. 262, where the foregoing examples will be found.
[2] *Hist. Hum. Mar.*, I, p. 441. [3] Loc. cit., p. 266. [4] Ibid., p. 265.

their ancestors in the remote past, but on what may happen to themselves in the future. As we saw in Chapter VII, there is no reason to believe that real blows in the distant past lead to magical shocks in the present. The dangers which a man fears from his mother-in-law are purely magical, and magical dangers never are, and never were, real dangers.

It seems to me that the custom of mother-in-law avoidance is connected with another widespread custom, that by which a man is not allowed intercourse with his wife except by stealth. 'One of the 'Japanese words for marriage is "yome-iri", which 'may be interpreted "to slip by night into the house ", 'and the expression accurately describes the mode of 'connubial intercourse among a large proportion of 'primitive peoples'.[1] Among the Khasis of Burma a man visited his mother-in-law's house, where his wife lived, after dark only, and did not eat there. Among the Nagas of Manipur the husband, until he becomes old, only visits his wife clandestinely after dark. The Tipperah of Bengal gains access to his wife's room like a burglar, and leaves it before dawn; and so do the Yakuts, Kurils, and Samoyeds of Siberia. A Tartar bridegroom is thrashed by his bride's brothers if they catch him leaving her room, and similar customs are observed by many tribes of Central Asia, Persia, and the Caucasus, and by the Akamba and other tribes of East and Central Africa. According to Plutarch the Spartan bridegroom slipped into his bride's house by night and 'having stayed with her a short time, he 'modestly retired to his usual apartment to sleep with 'the other young men; and he continued to observe

[1] Mothers, I, p. 513, where the following examples are to be found.

A MAN AND HIS MOTHER-IN-LAW

'the same caution afterwards, spending the day with
'his companions and reposing with them at night,
'and only visiting his bride with great caution and
'apprehension of being discovered by the rest of the
'family'. The Algonkin, Iroquois, and Assiniboin
only visited the dwellings of their wives by night, and
a Pueblo Indian was not allowed to enter his wife's
house till a child had been born, but slept with her
outside. The Bororos of Brazil live in the men's
common house, and only visit their wives by stealth.
Similar customs are reported of the Caribs, and also
from New Guinea, Fiji, and Borneo. Mr. Briffault, to
whose industry we owe this collection of facts, supposes
that all these customs are reminiscent of a time when
bridegrooms went in danger of death, or at any rate
of severe ill-treatment, from the relatives of their brides,
and he gives some cases in which they are still liable
to be roughly handled. As, however, I have said
before, when people put themselves to trouble and
inconvenience to avoid a danger, it is a danger in the
present and not in the remote past that they fear; it
is clear that in most of the cases quoted there is no
real danger, and therefore the danger they fear must
be a magical danger. We are not told who it is, in
particular, that the man must not see, but it is clear
that while the woman's male relatives may be absent,
at the men's common house, with other women, or
elsewhere, her mother will always be in the house with
her, and that it is by her that the husband must not
be seen. If this hypothesis is correct it is clear that
this custom is merely a form of mother-in-law avoidance,
and that the explanation of one will be the explanation
of the other.

CHAPTER XIX

HOW DID EXOGAMY ARISE?

WE have seen in the last three chapters that there are three taboos which the savage in many cases must be very careful to observe in his dealings with the opposite sex :

(1) He must not have intercourse with a woman of his own exogamous group.
(2) He must not see, or have anything to do with, a menstruous woman.
(3) He must not see, or have anything to do with, his mother-in-law.

We also saw that there is no good reason for believing that any of these taboos are founded either in nature or in reason ; they are genuine taboos, that is to say, magical prohibitions. There is another point to be noted : our knowledge of the peoples who now occupy the lowest rungs on the ladder of culture, such peoples as the jungle tribes of Malaya or the Pygmies of the Congo forest, is incomplete, but such as it is it suggests that these peoples either do not observe the three taboos which we have mentioned above, or observe them in a more or less rudimentary form. It might be supposed, in fact it has been supposed, that where we find a custom, rite, or taboo in a rudimentary form being observed by a people at a very low cultural level, we are justified in assuming that we have discovered the original form of that custom, etc. ; but a little consideration will show that this view is misleading.

HOW DID EXOGAMY ARISE? 123

We should have to suppose that the dual organization wherever we find it, is a development of group exogamy in the form in which we find it, for example, among the Bushmen of South Africa, who live in groups of about twenty persons. A man is not allowed to marry within his group, but must join another group, where the warmth of his welcome and the number of wives he obtains depend on his success as a hunter.[1]

Now just as we saw in Chapter IX that it is impossible to form a dual organization by taking a group of married persons and their children and dividing it into exogamous halves, so we must note here that it is equally impossible to form a dual organization out of a number of small exogamous groups. It would inevitably be found that some of Group A, for example, had married into Group B, of Group B into Group C, and of Group C into Group A. This difficulty can only be got over by supposing that in some mysterious and unexplained fashion the dual organization existed unofficially before it existed officially. It is also difficult to believe that a dual organization could arise among nomads; it could easily continue among nomads, once they had been divided into two exogamous moieties, but it is difficult to see how it could possibly arise except among a settled people; the system must have taken a long time to establish itself firmly, and meanwhile there must have been a ready means of distinguishing the tentative A's from the tentative B's, while they must at the same time have been near enough to make love to each other's women. I suggest that these conditions could only be fulfilled by settled people living on both banks of a stream.

[1] Mothers, I, p. 279.

The dual organization is found at the present day chiefly in the Pacific Islands and Australia, but there are records and survivals of it in India, Ceylon, Siam, and Cambodia, and in all these areas it is not merely concerned with the regulation of marriage, but fills a very important place in the religious and social life of the community.[1] It is the opinion of Mr. Hocart, and also of Dr. W. H. R. Rivers and Sir James Frazer [2] that cross-cousin marriage, the distribution of which we sketched in Chapter XVI, is an indication of the former existence of the dual organization. The evidence is by no means conclusive, but such as it is it suggests that the dual organization arose in the area of the ancient civilization, that is to say, the area between the Nile and the Indus, at an early, but not very early, stage in the development of human culture.

At the present stage of our knowledge it is impossible to do more than make a guess at the origin of the dual organization, but I shall venture to adopt this course, and for two reasons; the first is that my guess may contain a germ of truth, and the second is that having criticized the theories of so many distinguished writers, I feel that it would be cowardly not to give other people a chance to criticize me.

I shall begin by assuming that the three taboos which are mentioned at the beginning of this chapter are connected, and further that since the taboo on menstruous women is the simplest in every way, it is probably the oldest. I suppose that men became more and more frightened of menstruous women till they did not feel safe unless they had some obstacle between them and

---

[1] A. M. Hocart, *Ceylon Journal of Science*, February 1928.
[2] FOT, II, p. 222.

HOW DID EXOGAMY ARISE?

the women as a whole, and for this purpose utilized the stream on whose banks they lived; all the men lived on one side, and merely visited the women on the other, taking with them some of the spoils of the chase. This would not last for very long; old men would stay with the women, and old women with the men, and the idea might gradually arise that it was safe for people of both sexes to live on the same side so long as they did not have sexual intercourse. There was as yet no individual marriage—the divine king and queen were the first pair to be married—but the men would tend to visit the same women, those nearest to them on the opposite bank, and these would often be in fact their cross-cousins, though the relationship was not yet recognized: when individual marriage came into existence, cross-cousins were the people between whom it could be most easily arranged, if the rule of exogamy was to be observed.

All this time, we may suppose, the belief in ancestral spirits had been slowly developing, and the danger from a breach of the menstrual taboo, which had formerly been supposed to come from the women themselves, or their blood, was in part transferred to the spirits, who thus became jealous guardians of the taboo. The women were secluded during their period, and old women were set to guard them. Accidents, however, sometimes happen, and spirits are just as angry at accidental as at deliberate breaches of taboo, so as a measure of precaution the old women, who kept a real watch in the menstrual period, kept a ritual watch at other times. A man from the other side was safe, because he could get safely back across the stream before the spirits, who are never very quick-witted, had realized what had happened, so all the ill-luck fell on the woman's own relatives. If the man from the other side did not obtrude himself on the old woman's notice, they could assure the spirits that they were not parties to his actions; but if he did obtrude himself he was bringing trouble upon them and so was lucky if he got away with a whole skin. Eventually, when individual marriage was evolved, the individual mother-in-law replaced the old women of the group.

The theory which I have outlined, and which could of course be developed in much greater detail, may seem fantastic, but that does not prove its falsity. I do not claim that it is true, for it is merely a guess, but I do claim that it is an improvement on previous theories in two respects; in the first place it attempts to account for all the features of the three early sexual taboos and not merely a few selected features of one selected taboo and secondly it does not demand a sudden breach with the past, a thing which never happens either in savage or in civilized communities except under foreign influence.

Is there any evidence in its favour? Not much, perhaps, but there is some. We have seen that menstruous women must not cross streams; in many folk-stories we are told that witches cannot cross running water, and we may perhaps equate witch with malignant old woman, and thus with mother-in-law. A man who has had intercourse no longer crosses a stream, but he often takes care to avoid trouble from the evil spirits by performing a ritual ablution, and water, especially running or 'living' water, is generally regarded as a powerful magical disinfectant. There

HOW DID EXOGAMY ARISE?

is a widespread class of magical rites in which the hands must be washed after touching the sacred objects.

There are still a few cases in which exogamous moieties are separated by water; 'the Kombees of the 'Kutree caste, who live on both banks of the river 'Myhee, are divided by it into classes. The higher 'class destroy their daughters, in order that their 'sons may be forced to go to the other side of the river 'for wives, and receive in return large dowries'.[1]

Mr. Hocart tells me that the villages of Tumbou and Moala, in the Lau Islands of Fiji, are divided by water into moieties which were formerly exogamous, and that the Sâkya and Kôli, the two families who formed the traditional ancestry of Buddha, lived on opposite banks of the river Rohâna.

The houses of the King and Queen of Uganda had to be separated by a running stream.[2]

Among some of the tribes of California the exogamous moieties are called 'downstream' and 'upstream', or 'land' and 'water'.[3]

' When the whole tribe is gathered together on some 'ceremonial occasion, the two pairs of sub-classes will 'camp on opposite sides of a creek,' wrote Mr. Howitt of certain tribes of Victoria.[4]

Mr. Torday[5] tells us that 'among the Western 'Bantu the maternal soul goes (at death) to the clan 'ancestors underground, while the paternal soul joins 'the gens ancestors under or near the water'. Why should the paternal soul go to the water unless the father was supposed to come from the water?

[1] Browne, *Infanticide in India*, p. 56.
[2] J. Roscoe, *The Baganda*, p. 203.   [3] A. L. Kroeber, op. cit., p. 494.
[4] A. W. Howitt, *The Native Tribes of South-East Australia*, p. 14.
[5] E. Torday in JRAI, 1928, 242. See also note p. 197.

There is one thread which must now be picked up ; I suggested in Chapter VII that sham marriage by capture was connected with mother-in-law avoidance, and we can now see how the former custom may have arisen. I have suggested that fear of a breach of the menstrual taboo gradually developed into a belief that the ancestral spirits did not like the women of the group to be touched by strangers ; that ritual precautions were taken to deceive the spirits ; and that the most important of these precautions was that a man, when visiting the opposite group, must not allow himself to be seen by the old women of that group. Now, when individual marriage came into existence, and later on, for reasons which I shall suggest presently, became patrilocal instead of matrilocal, the spirits, who had strongly objected to their women's having intercourse with strangers, might be supposed to object even more strongly to their removal. Whether this be so or not, it is clear that the rites are, in the main, of the same character ; in one case the man has to gain access to the young woman without being seen by her relatives, and is maltreated if he fails, and in the other he must try to remove her without being seen by her relatives, and is maltreated if he fails ; but in the latter case the rite, since it takes place once for all, tends to be of a more elaborate and more violent character. In many cases the ritual resistance of the bride and her relatives ceases at a certain point ; I suggest that this was originally the point at which water was reached.

It may be asked whether it is possible that such a group of customs originating in one area could spread all over the world ; it does not appear that all these customs have spread quite all over the world, since

HOW DID EXOGAMY ARISE?

some of the most primitive peoples seem never to have fully acquired them. It may have been a pure accident that the tribe which developed these customs succeeded in obtaining the mastery over its neighbours; it may be that these customs were an accidental consequence of that denser settlement in favourable areas which led to civilization; it may be that, though purely irrational in origin, they happened to have some sociological value. If we believed that customs only come into existence and survive because they are the best possible, we ought hastily to reimpose the mother-in-law taboo upon ourselves.

CHAPTER XX

THE DIFFUSION OF CULTURE

IN the last chapter we saw reason to believe that the customs which we find among the most primitive peoples were not the invention of those peoples, but were copied from or imposed by peoples of higher culture, usually in a modified form. This process is known as the diffusion of culture, and since all the theories which I have or shall put forward depend on such diffusion, it will perhaps be as well to deal with it before considering how the various complicated and illogical incest laws which we find in different parts of the world developed from a system of simple exogamy.

During the latter half of the last century it was widely believed that the resemblances in culture, both moral and material, which we find among widely separated peoples, were due to the simple fact that in similar circumstances the human mind always works in a similar way. If polished stone axes and a horror of menstrual blood are found, as they are found, in the most remote corners of the globe, this, it was supposed, was because the human mind, confronted with blood or a stone, will always react in a similar manner. The functional anthropologists have carried this theory still further; not only does man always react similarly in similar circumstances, but such reaction is always characterized by the maximum of wisdom and foresight. Polished stone axes are everywhere the same because man was everywhere determined to make the

THE DIFFUSION OF CULTURE 131

best use of his material, and succeeded in so doing; horror of menstrual blood is the highest wisdom, because it leads to sexual purity or social cohesion or some other virtue which the early ancestors of all existing peoples foresaw would be essential for the preservation of the species.

Such views are open to serious objection, in the first place because they attempt to explain the resemblances in culture, yet make no attempt to explain the differences in culture. If the reactions of the human mind are always similar, how is it that the results are often so strikingly dissimilar? Why, for example, was human sacrifice so unevenly distributed, and why are we not all allowed the same number of wives? The second objection to the theory is that it postulates for the human race as a whole a foresight, an adaptability and an originality which it is a matter of everyday experience that it does not possess; finally, though history is nothing but a record of the movements of races and cultures, we are invited to suppose that in prehistoric times such movements never occurred, and to believe that nobody could possibly have crossed the Torres Straits from the time when the blacks originally entered Australia till its discovery by Europeans.

The 'independent inventionists', as they might be called, make little or no attempt to answer these and other criticisms; like all upholders of ancient fallacies they claim the right to throw the burden of proof upon their opponents, who are, however, quite ready to bear it.

The scientific study of early material culture and its comparison with the existing cultures of savages was inaugurated by Sir E. B. Tylor and General Pitt-Rivers in the middle of the last century. Since then a careful comparison of artifacts from various parts of the world has enabled students to realize the very large number of steps required to produce even simple artifacts, such as stone axes, and the correspondingly large number of coincidences which would be required to produce the same artifact separately in two independent cultures. Those who have not studied the question are apt to be misled by the simultaneous discovery of improvements to machinery in different parts of the Western world, since they do not realize that Europe and America are parts of the same culture complex, and that one coincidence where people are intentionally working on the same lines is a very different matter from a score of coincidences where they are not.

As an illustration I will take the practice of mummification, since not only does it bring out the points which I have just been trying to make, but it also shows the connexion which must always exist between moral and material culture, and I shall quote one of the most distinguished authorities on the subject, Dr. H. S. Harrison : [1]

' A third example is that of mummification, which has
' been dealt with faithfully by Professor Elliot Smith.
' The assumption is often made that mummification
' originated in more than one part of the world, as a
' result of the observation that under conditions of
' aridity the bodies of the dead suffered desiccation
' instead of decay ; and that this observation readily
' led to the evolution of processes of preservation by
' artificial means. That this is merely an assumption
' is obvious. . . . That under certain conditions the

[1] Presidential Address to Section H, British Association, 1929.

'body, buried or unburied, did not entirely lose its
'human semblance, was in itself no inducement to the
'conservation of the dried remains. A shrunken body
'was of no more value than a skeleton, and new views
'of man's place in nature, and in supernature, had to
'be evolved before the preservation of the body became
'a means to an end. . . . For the idea to originate in
'two or more regions independently, there must have
'been coincidences in social and religious sequences, as
'well as in natural environment. For the independent
'evolution of artificial preservation out of natural
'desiccation there would be needed further coincidences
'in the growth of the idea of preventing the decay of
'animal or human flesh, and of the means and methods
'of prevention; and finally, in so far as there is
'agreement in different parts of the world in the tech-
'nique of preparing the body for the embalming
'process, there must be assumed still more coinci-
'dences, some of them significantly trivial.'

Professor Elliot Smith, who may be regarded as the founder of the modern diffusionist school, was the first to point out the coincidences to which Dr. Harrison alludes; mummification is, or has been, practised extensively in the Canary Islands, in India and Further India, in Melanesia, and in many parts of Australia and America, and Professor Elliot Smith is convinced that in all these areas mummification was derived from Egypt. Mr. Warren R. Dawson, who has made an intensive study of the subject, confirms this view. He tells us,[1] among many other facts, that part of the Egyptian process of embalming consisted in macerating the corpse in a strong saline solution, which caused the

[1] JRAI, 1928, p. 117.

epidermis to peel off. The Australian blacks, and certain tribes of South America which practised mummification, did not macerate the corpse, but were nevertheless at great pains to scrape off the epidermis; 'they perpetuated a custom which for them had neither 'purpose nor use, a clear indication that the practice 'was borrowed from elsewhere'. In Australia 'mum-'mification was practised even when the corpse was 'destined for cremation', which 'suggests that the 'custom was borrowed and followed as a mere ritual 'practice that had neither a utilitarian purpose to 'serve, nor could it have been prompted by the motives 'that originally gave rise to the art of embalming— 'i.e. to preserve the corpse indefinitely from decay, 'and to perpetuate the identity of the individual. A 'parallel instance is provided by Burma, where the 'bodies of royal personages and priests are elaborately 'embalmed and then cremated'.

The idea of cremation seems to be that the deceased ascends to heaven in the smoke, and though the Hindu theologians succeeded in combining the rites of mummification and cremation in the dogma that unless the body was purified before being burnt it could not be reanimated,[1] it is clear that the two rites are really distinct and inconsistent. The 'independent inventionists' must then suppose not merely that the Australian blacks independently took all the moral and material steps which led the ancient Egyptians to the development of mummification, but that they also took all the steps which led in Asia to the development of cremation, and finally that they independently combined the two rites in exactly the same way as did the Hindus.

[1] Mary Levin, 'Mummification and Cremation in India,' *Man*, 1930, 48.

As a fact, however, their technique was not a copy of the Egyptian, but merely an inferior imitation, and as they never properly grasped the technique, so we may well believe that they never really grasped the ideas upon which that technique was based. Just as there are to-day few savages whose culture has not been to some extent influenced by Christianity or Islam, so, in all probability, have the religious ideas current in the centres of civilization always tended to spread outwards, becoming more and more superficial as they got farther from contact with their centres of distribution. There are many discoveries and inventions, both in the realm of ideas and in that of artifacts, of which we can say with certainty that they were made in one area, and in one area only; there is not a single idea or artifact of which we can say with certainty that it was discovered or invented in two areas independently. Magic is very ancient, and its history is for the most part unknown, but arguing from the known to the unknown we may conclude that the probability that any magical rite was devised in two different places is exceedingly remote, and that if the incest taboo was evolved from magical ideas, or practices, each of these originated in some one area, not necessarily the same one. There is no more justification for assuming that the natives of Central Africa invented the magical rites which they now practise than there is for assuming that they invented the bicycles which they now ride.

CHAPTER XXI

WHAT IS A MYTH?

IN attempting to account for the origin of exogamy our evidence is limited to actual survivals in the customs of existing peoples. The laws of incest, however, especially those of civilized peoples, though they are in all probability based on exogamy, introduce two new principles—that a child is a blood-relation to his father, and therefore cannot marry, e.g. his father's sister, and that a man is a blood-relation to his wife, and therefore cannot marry, e.g. his wife's sister. In attempting to discover how these two principles arose we have, in addition to existing laws and customs, a large number of incest myths, the explanation of which, if we can find it, is bound to throw light upon the problem, since these myths, though in many cases extremely ancient, are later than the introduction of exogamy, before which, as we have seen, there could have been no incest.

Since, however, the value attached to the evidence of myths must depend on what is understood by a myth, it will first be necessary to define the term.

Apart from the psycho-analysts, who produce myths from the sub-conscious much as conjurors produce rabbits from hats, there are four theories of the origin of myths :

(1) The first theory is that apparently favoured by Dr. Marett, when he speaks (as we saw on page 64) of ' composing ' a myth. The belief that myths were composed by imaginative persons to instil a moral idea,

account for an obscure custom, or amuse a leisure hour was once widely held, but until I read Dr. Marett's words I had supposed it to be extinct among those who have made a serious study of the subject.

(2) The second theory, which arose in the nineteenth century, is the Naturalistic, which supposes that myths are due to a practice of explaining the movements of the heavenly bodies, the cycle of the seasons, and the growth and decay of vegetation in terms of human activities. This theory no doubt contains an element of truth, since the sun, moon, etc., appear as human beings in many myths, and their appearance has to be explained; but the mistake of the theory lies in the assumption that the savage is consumed with a desire to explain the phenomena of nature. As a fact, he is not in the least interested in them, except in so far as they affect him personally, and even then he never wants to know why, or if he does his curiosity is satisfied with the most trifling explanation.

(3) The third theory is the Euhemeristic, according to which all myths are more or less distorted accounts of actual historical events. It is associated with the late Sir William Ridgeway, who, in his *Origin of Tragedy*, attempted to show that all gods are dead men, and that all myths are more or less garbled versions of their actual doings. Sir James Frazer takes a similar view when he [1] speaks of ' the miraculous ' features which gather round the memory of popular ' heroes, as naturally as moss and lichens gather about ' stones '. There are exceptions, but generally speaking this is quite untrue; Alfred the Great and William the Conqueror were popular heroes, yet nobody ever

[1] FOT, III, p. 97.

accused either of them of performing a miracle; exceptions only occur when real people become confused in tradition with gods or mythical heroes.

The objections to the theory are, first, that, like the theory of commemoration criticized in Chapter VII, it attaches an improbable importance to what are assumed to be isolated incidents in human history, and secondly that it compels us to suppose that the same strange accidents and adventures happened to heroes all over the world, and were given the same prominence in myth. Frazer himself gives a list,[1] which could easily be extended, of heroes who had a narrow escape from death shortly after birth, and it is easy to compile similar lists of heroes who triumphed over dragons or disappeared mysteriously from hill-tops. Coincidence can hardly be stretched to cover all these cases. 'The 'Euhemerists', says Mr. Hocart,[2] 'came nearer the 'truth in so far as they recognized that the prime 'interest of man has always been man; so they looked 'to human actions to explain myths. Where they 'erred was in limiting themselves to those actions which 'are least capable of making a deep impression on 'tradition, that is transient events enacted once for 'all. At the time a great battle, a tragedy of the palace, 'the sad fate of lovers may fill men's minds, but after 'the first blaze these sensations go out, while customs 'continue to smoulder on during the ages.'

(4) The theory that the clue to myth is to be found in custom, or rather in ritual, which is magical custom, first adumbrated by Professor Durkheim, was developed by that brilliant scholar, the late Miss Jane Harrison, in her *Themis*. It is impossible to discuss in a small

[1] FOT, II, p. 437. [2] *Ceylon Journal of Science*, February 1928.

WHAT IS A MYTH?

space all Miss Harrison's conclusions, which I believe to be generally sound, but I will try to illustrate them by an example, of which she might or might not have approved.

The Lord Mayor of London is, in the opinion of Londoners, a far more august and powerful personage than the elderly business man who annually takes the part, and his ' Show' even now almost assumes the character of a religious rite, inaugurating the annual reincarnation of a civic deity. If there were no written records and no fixed religious dogmas, it might in time come to be believed that the Lord Mayor, who had ruled over the city from time immemorial, was the divine hero who had founded the city, and that the annual occupant of the office was merely his representative. This would be merely a development of the universal tendency for an office to transcend the personality of the office-holder. Each successive holder of the office would have to do exactly what his predecessor had done, and in order that there might be no mistake, all the traditional acts would be annually recited by certain elders whose duty it would be to memorize them. The narrative so recited would be the myth of the Lord Mayor, and could be described indifferently as an account of what the divine hero originally did, or of what his representative annually does. The myth is full of miracles because the ritual is full of magic miracles; the Lord Mayor gives a lavish ' Show ', and thereby causes the city to prosper; he ascends the bench, and thereby assures justice to all citizens; he is girt with a sword, and thereby defeats single-handed the city's enemies.

If, however, the Corporation were to be overthrown

by a revolution, what would happen to the Lord Mayor? Having lasted for a thousand years, and having during that period played a part in the life of every member of the community, he would not, like the hero of an hour or the event of a day, be speedily forgotten, but would long linger in tradition, and that tradition would be a myth. He would become a legendary hero, who by the aid of his magical powers was able miraculously to help his friends and defeat his enemies, and by the Euhemerists he would be reduced to the status of a historical character; they would argue about his actual date, but would have no doubt that the miracles, which are really the central feature of the myth, were later additions.

Myth, then, is never fictitious, since it is always the story of something that real people do or did; on the other hand, it is never historical, because it is always the story of something which was done not once but many times. Myth and ritual are complementary; ritual is a magic drama to which myth is the book of the words, which often survives after the drama has ceased to be performed. But there is this to be noted—in a magic drama, as in its descendant the stage drama, there are certain things which the actors do, and others which they merely pretend to do. We know, for example, when we read that 'Hamlet makes a pass through the 'arras. . . . Polonius falls and dies', that Hamlet will really make a pass, but that Polonius will not really die. We know of rites which included a human sacrifice, and of other rites in which there was, and is, a make-believe human sacrifice, yet the myth is the same in both cases. Incest myths are stories of an incest rite, but when we come to consider them we shall

WHAT IS A MYTH?

have to consider whether the incest was real or make-believe; this is a point of some importance.

There are hundreds of these incest myths, and when we come to examine them we find to our surprise that they are all very much of a pattern. In a great many cases the incest myth forms part of a creation myth, and in all, or nearly all, of the remainder we find features which suggest that it once did so. A creation myth is a story which purports to tell how the world was first made and peopled, and usually includes a number of features such as a flood, the death of a man or god, the creation of a man and woman from clay, an act of incest, and the creation of a new race. It was formerly supposed that these stories represented the attempts of primitive philosophers to account for the origin of the universe, and what were supposed to be their weird imaginings caused surprise. Bearing in mind, however, that a myth is the story of a rite, we can now see that these myths are really stories of creation rites, and not attempts to explain anything. Why should there be creation rites? Because it is widely held, and has been from time immemorial, that in order to keep the world up to the mark it is necessary to create it, or rather re-create it, either at regular intervals or in times of trouble.

The Karok of California call their New Year ceremony 'world-making'.[1] Mr. Hocart tells us [2] that the Fijians, when the crops are bad, have a ceremony which they call 'creating the earth'; that the Hindu scriptures describe at great length the method to be followed for the creation of the world; that the Pharaoh was able to renew every day 'the mystery of creation';

---

[1] A. L. Kroeber, op. cit., p. 102.   [2] *Kingship*, pp. 190 seq.

and that the Eleusinian Mysteries included a ceremony in which the hierophant took the part of the ' creator '.

According to the Hindus, the gods slew Purusha, divided him up, and formed from his head and limbs the universe, making the sky from his head, the sun from his eye, and so on. In the same way, according to our Nordic ancestors, the gods slew Ymir, made the sky of his skull, the clouds of his brains, and so on. ' Is it credible ', Mr. Hocart asks, ' that man should 'have speculated and speculated as to the origin of 'things, and as the result of it all come to the extra- 'ordinary conclusion that the hills were made out of 'a giant's bones, and the clouds out of his brains ? Is 'it not much easier to believe . . . that the ancient 'Germans merely put on record the details of a 'human sacrifice ? We can understand how such a 'sacrifice having travelled about the world should have 'similar memories behind it in remotely distant places. 'But if these myths are merely the outcome of wild 'and uncontrolled imaginings, how do we explain 'the remarkable agreement of the modern Gilbert 'Islanders with the ancient Indians and Germans ? 'The islanders relate that Na Arean slew his father 'with the latter's consent, took his right eye and flung 'it to the Eastern sky, where it became the sun ; the 'left eye and flung it to the Western sky, and behold ! 'the moon.' And so on with the rest of his body. ' If ', says Mr. Hocart, ' we explain creation myths as 'memories, more or less accurate, of creation ceremonies, 'we have no need to postulate a mind differently 'constituted from any we are acquainted with.'

Since this was written Professor Daryll Forde has published his account of the Yuma Indians of

WHAT IS A MYTH?

Colorado [1], who not only still perform a creation ceremony, but fail to make a clear distinction between the rite and the myth: 'Informants tend constantly to refer 'to the activities of the existing rite in terms of the 'original. The Yuma, in other words, does not clearly 'distinguish between the mythological foundation and 'the existing ceremonial'. If the myth is derived from the rite this is of course what we should expect, but it seems impossible to account for it otherwise. The rite is now held annually; its object is to restore strength to the community, and especially to the relatives of those who have died since the last ceremony. The myth begins with the death of the creator god, Kukumat, caused by his offended daughter Frog. He is cremated, and thenceforward the myth follows the rite, which is a very elaborate one lasting for four days, except that certain borrowings which have recently been added to the ritual have not yet become established in the myth, which is again exactly what we should expect. The Marindineeze of Dutch New Guinea have also a creation rite with a corresponding creation myth.[2]

If, then, as appears to be well established, a creation myth is nothing but the story of a creation rite, we must conclude that where we find incest as part of the creation myth, incest, real or make-believe, formed part of the creation rite; and, further than that, since we have reason to believe that all creation rites are derived from one original creation rite, it seems impossible to avoid the conclusion that all incest rites, and consequently all incest myths, are derived from one original incest rite.

[1] C. Daryll Forde, *Ethnography of the Yuma Indians*, p. 214.
[2] FOT, I, p. 39.

CHAPTER XXII

INCEST IN MYTH AND RITUAL

WE saw in the last chapter that the creation myth is a long and complex one, and that the various forms in which it appears are probably all derived from a common source. We are not here concerned with the myth as a whole, since my object is simply to show that the incest myth is an integral part of the creation myth, or, in other words, that an incest rite formed part of the original creation rite.

Mr. Hocart, in the chapter from which I quoted, has only dealt with certain aspects of the myth, and has therefore not mentioned the important fact that before you can create a new world, you must destroy the old one. Bearing this fact in mind, let us try to reduce the creation myth, in so far as it concerns our purpose, to the simplest possible terms:

(a) The world is overwhelmed by a flood, and the inhabitants drowned.
(b) The gods slay a giant, and from his flesh and bones make a new world.
(c) The gods create a human pair, brother and sister, and place them in the world.
(d) At the instigation of the sister the pair unite, and
(e) Become the ancestors of a new race of men.

What was actually done, I suggest, was as follows:

(a) Last year's images and the remains of last year's victim were thrown into the water.

(b) A human victim (last year's brother) was killed and dismembered, and his flesh and bones arranged in a conventional pattern.

(c) Two images, male and female, were made from clay and the victim's blood, and set in the midst of the pattern.

(d) A girl (the queen-sister) approached a youth (the king-brother), and the pair united.

(e) All the people rejoiced because they and the world had been created afresh.

Before considering the evidence of the myths, there is one point to be noted—before animating the first pair the creator in many cases makes several, usually two, unsuccessful attempts. Thus the Kumis of Chittagong [1] say that the creator made images from clay every day, but every night a great snake devoured them; at last he set a dog to guard the images, and was then able to complete the creation. The Mundas, a tribe of Chota Nagpur, say that the sun-god made clay figures of a man and a woman, but they were trampled by a horse; the god set a spider to guard them, and the spider wove a web round them in such a way that the horse could not break them; the god was then able to endow them with life. In a legend of the Dusuns of Borneo the creator made figures first of stone and then of wood, but was unable to animate them; at last he tried with clay, and succeeded.[2] The Michoacans of Mexico say that the great god Tucapacha made a man and a woman out of clay, but when they bathed in the river the clay fell to

---

[1] In this chapter all references, unless otherwise stated, are to FOT, Chapters I and IV.

[2] O. Rutter, *The Pagans of North Borneo*, p. 228.

pieces ; he tried with ashes, but the result was the same ; finally he tried metal, and they were then watertight, and by their union became the progenitors of mankind. I have found no evidence to suggest what was the nature of the rite corresponding to this myth ; it does not seem to have occurred in Egypt, where Khnoumou, Father of the Gods, moulded men out of clay on his potter's wheel, nor in Babylonia, where the god Bel cut off his own head, and the other gods caught the blood, mixed it with earth, and fashioned men from the paste. It does not seem to have reached Uganda, where a rationalized version of the story is told, in which an early king was thrown into a clay-pit at birth, but saved by the potter.[1] There seems, however, to be a reminiscence of the myth in the Genesis story of Cain, Abel, and Seth, and we shall meet it again presently.

Egypt being, as far as we know at present, the earliest centre from which culture was diffused, it is there that we should first look for a creation myth, and we find not one but a succession.[2] In the first, Khepera found himself in the midst of an ocean ; after giving being to himself by uttering his own name he created Shu and Tefnunt ; they were united and produced Nut the sky-goddess and Keb the earth-god. Nut remained in the sky by day, but at night she descended and rested on the body of her brother Keb, by whom she had a large family of gods. Khepera seems to have made the sun and moon out of his eyes, and created man by placing his members together and shedding tears on them.

[1] J. Roscoe, *The Baganda*, p. 215.
[2] E. A. Wallis Budge, *Legends of the Gods*.

In the second myth Ra is angry with mankind, so he sends forth his eye in the form of Hathor to destroy them, and then floods the 'meadows of the Four 'Heavens' with beer. Later Isis causes Ra to be killed by a serpent; his eyes become the sun and moon, his heart is taken from his body, and Isis gets possession of his secret name.

In the third myth it was Osiris who was killed, and his sister Isis ' made to rise up the helpless members of ' him whose heart was at rest, she drew from him his ' essence, and she made therefrom an heir '. She performed this feat in the form of a hawk, and the heir was Horus, who collected Osiris's members. According to another version Osiris's body was divided into fourteen parts, which were collected by Isis.

It will be noted that there is a flood in two, an act of incest in two, and the dividing up of a human victim in all three of these myths, while the creation of the first human beings from clay appears in the myth cited above.

As regards ritual, we know that throughout the historic period it was orthodox for the Pharaoh to marry his sister, and that he often married his mother and daughters as well. Intercourse between the king and queen formed a definite part of the religious ritual.[1] In the love-poems, which were probably ritual hymns, the lovers invariably address each other as brother and sister.

In Greece, Dronus and Rhea were brother and sister, and Zeus and Hera were their children. Cronus mutilated his father Uranus, and both he and Zeus were worshipped with human sacrifice. There are

[1] G. Elliott Smith, *Human History*, p. 310.

incest stories of other gods; in a hymn Artemis describes herself as the wife, sister, and daughter of Apollo;[1] Dionysus was torn to pieces by the Titans; and Semele consumed his heart, whence he was born again of her,[2] so that in a sense he was both her husband and her son.

In the Thesmophoria, an Athenian creation rite, the remains of the previous year's victims played an important part.[3]

There are several Greek flood myths. In the best-known one the sole survivors are Deucalion and Pyrrha, who though not brother and sister are ortho-cousins; they are instructed to throw their mother's bones behind their backs, and throw stones, which turn into men and women. Deucalion was the son of Prometheus who made men and women from clay, also after the human race had been destroyed by a flood.

In a Lithuanian myth the sole local survivors of a great flood were a man and woman too old to produce children; by the direction of a god they jumped nine times over the bones of the earth, and each jump produced a couple who became the ancestors of a Lithuanian tribe.

In Norse mythology the same elements repeatedly appear. We saw in the last chapter that the gods killed the giant Ymir, and made a new world from his flesh and bones; his blood became a flood, which drowned all the giants except Bergelmir and his wife. The gods found two inanimate human forms, and animated them; they were the ancestors of mankind. Njord the sky-god marries his sister the earth-goddess,

[1] L. R. Farnell, *Cults of the Greek States*, II, p. 466.
[2] E. S. Hartland, *Primitive Paternity*, I, p. 18.
[3] L. R. Farnell, op. cit., III, p. 89.

INCEST IN MYTH AND RITUAL

and their children are Frey and Freya. There are a stone giant and a clay giant, which Thor smashes to pieces. Finally at Ragnarok all the gods are killed and the world destroyed; the sole survivors are a youth and a maiden, Lif and Lifthrasir, who become the ancestors of mankind.[1] To another Norse myth we shall allude presently.

From Ireland we learn that the two sons of Partholon married their two sisters.[2] Lugaid was the son of Clothru by her three brothers; he became high king of Ireland, married his mother, and was succeeded by their son, Crimthann. Lugaid's peculiarity was that he had two circular red lines on his skin, one round his neck and the other round his waist; they marked off the portions of his body in which he resembled his three fathers.[3] It is possible that we have here a reminiscence of a time when instead of the king's being actually killed and dismembered, a ritual pretence of so doing was made; the ritual wounding of a man, usually followed by the sacrifice of an animal, occurred in ancient Greece, and still occurs in various parts of the world.[4]

Many survivals of the creation ritual are found in Europe in the Carnival, the May-Day festivities and other rites, but it does not appear that they throw any fresh light on the problem we are considering, and we will therefore pass to Asia, and will deal first with the Arab story of Bu Zeid, the legendary hero of the Beni Hilal.[5] He refuses to impregnate his wife, so the tribesmen, who wish their sheikh to have an heir, induce his sister to go to his bed unknown to

[1] Wagner and McDowall, *Asgard and the Gods*.
[2] Jubainville, *Irish Mythological Cycle*, p. 19.   [3] Ibid., pp. 206, 212.
[4] GB, IV, pp. 214 seq.   [5] Bertram Thomas, *Arabia Felix*, p. 219.

him. At the critical moment she sticks a bodkin into him, and the result is the hero 'Azîz bin Khâlu ("'Azîz the son of his mother's brother"). The bodkin incident has a curious variant in Borneo, to which we shall come presently. The other incidents in the story are to be found in the Volsunga Saga; all the Volsungs are killed except Sigmund and his sister Signy; the latter goes to his bed in disguise, and the result is the hero Sinfjotli. But the parallel does not end there; Bu Zeid sets his wife's two sons to making bread, and they fail; Sigmund sets the two sons of Signy by her husband to making bread, and they fail; in each case the son of brother and sister tries last and succeeds. I suggest that the unsuccessful sons were the Creator's unsuccessful attempts. The myth of Arthur is very similar; by his sister, who visits him, and whom he does not know to be his sister, he becomes the father of Mordred.[1]

Mr. Thomas also tells us of a South Arabian rite by which a newly circumcised youth is (or was) chased three times round the circle of spectators by an unveiled maiden who is (or was) often his sister.[2]

The Yezîdîs of Mesopotamia have a curious variant of the myth, but one in which most of the features are clearly recognizable. Al-Hallâj is beheaded, and his head is thrown into the Tigris; his sister is filling her jar in the river when his soul comes floating down, and enters the jar. After drinking the water she becomes pregnant, and gives birth to a son.[3] With this we may compare an Egyptian story of how a girl became pregnant by eating a leaf from a tree which

---

[1] Malory, *Morte Darthur*, pp. 42–4. [2] JRAI, 1929, p. 102.
[3] R. H. W. Empson, *The Cult of the Peacock Angel*, p. 78.

INCEST IN MYTH AND RITUAL

grew on a dung-hill where her father's bones had been thrown.[1]

The Babylonian stories, in addition to the Bel myth already mentioned, tell us how the gods created the world by killing and cutting up the female monster, Tiamat.

At Hierapolis, on the Euphrates, there was a rite as a part of which a man spent seven days on the top of an obelisk; the alleged object of this was to show how men had climbed mountains and trees to escape from the flood.

Passing to India, we learn that according to one myth Yama, the Hindu god of the dead, had a twin sister Yami, and there is a hymn in which she proposes to him that they shall cohabit in order to perpetuate the species.[2] With this we may compare the Song of Solomon, probably a ritual hymn, in which the sister-lover is represented as seeking her brother, and also the Egyptian love-poems already mentioned.

According to another Hindu myth, Manu was the sole survivor of a flood; he offered a sacrifice of butter, curds, etc., and from the sacrifice grew a girl, who called herself his daughter, but became by him the mother of the human race.

The legendary founders of Buddha's clan were four brothers who married their four sisters.[3]

Many of the wild tribes of India have creation myths in which a brother and sister appear as the sole survivors of a flood, and become the parents of the race; they include the Bhils, the Mundas, and the Santals. According to the Kamars, this pair were

[1] E. S. Hartland, *Primitive Paternity*, I, p. 13.
[2] Dowson, *Dict. Hindu Mythology*.
[3] H. G. Q. Wales, *Siamese State Ceremonies*, p. 117.

the children of the first created pair. According to the Anals of Assam the sole survivors of the flood were a man and a woman who took refuge in a tree which grew at the top of a hill beside a large pond. Having spent the night in the tree, they found in the morning that they had been changed into tigers. The creator was apparently surprised at this, but hastened to create another couple, whom he empowered to kill the tigers and re-people the world.

Dr. Perry[1] has collected ten myths of incest from Indonesia and the adjacent regions, of which I will quote two. According to the Igorot of the Philippines the sole survivors of a flood were a brother and sister; the brother sees fire on the mountain-top, and when he summons up courage to go there finds his sister, who receives him with open arms. They were the ancestors of the Igorot.

One version of the Toradja (Celebes) creation myth states that the first pair of human beings descended from the sky; after a daughter had been born to them they quarrelled and separated, but later the woman wanted the man, and after some searching found him. They then had a son, and the son and daughter married and became the ancestors of the Toradja. According to another version the sole survivor of the flood was a pregnant woman; she gave birth to a son, who became her husband.

A myth of the Dayaks of Borneo tells how some people killed and cut up a large serpent, which until the flood began to flow they mistook for a tree; this caused the flood, of which the sole survivor was a woman. Having no husband, she took the fire-drill

[1] W. J. Perry, *Megalithic Cultures of Indonesia*, p. 100.

for mate, and had a son who had only half a head and body, and only one arm and leg. Eventually, however, he induced the wind to supply the missing parts.

The Dusuns of North Borneo have a story of a princess who became pregnant by falling on top of a prince in a pool of water; she had a son and daughter who became the ancestors of the Dusuns. The Muruts of the same region say that after the flood only a woman and her brother were left. He saw two squirrels mating, and asked her what it meant; she explained, and told him it was pleasant. They produced first a dog, and afterwards a son and daughter who married. According to another version the youth solicits his sister; she tells him that he must only pretend, but while so doing he is stung behind by a wasp; the resulting twins were the parents of mankind.[1] This version seems to be a variant of the Arab story given above.

The myths of the Malayan jungle tribes are similar, but we may note that in one case the first man emerges from the stem of a giant bamboo, and in another the moon is created after the flood.[2]

In a Formosan myth a brother and sister are the sole survivors of a flood; they unite and have a large family, but to mitigate the dangers of incest, keep a mat between them on the marriage bed. Among some of the Plains Indians of North America, it may be noted, newly married couples have to keep a hide between them on the marriage bed. According to another Formosan myth the custom of head-hunting was started by the survivors of a flood, who amused

---

[1] O. Rutter, *The Pagan Tribes of North Borneo*, p. 248.
[2] Skeat and Blagden, *Pagan Races of the Malay Peninsula*, pp. 185, 187.

themselves by cutting off the head of a bad boy, and hoisting it on a bamboo.

Fu-Hi, the legendary founder of Chinese civilization, instituted marriage at the instigation of his sister-wife Niu-Kua.[1]

In Japan the cult-hero Izanagi marries his sister Izanami; they achieve this by performing the ceremony of going round the pillar, and meeting face to face.[2]

In Siam the coronation ceremony seems to be a regular creation rite. The king used to marry his full sister, and it is now apparently the proper thing for him to marry his half-sister, but he prefers not to do so, as he must treat her with very great deference.[3] On the death of a king, his body is placed in an urn, and kept there till the bones are quite dry. They are then taken out and arranged in the form of a skeleton, and the king and nobles pour coco-nut water over them. They are taken to the place of cremation in a boat-shaped car, behind which ride two young princes. Formerly the ashes were jettisoned in midstream.[4] The resemblance between these rites and those of the Shiluk of the Upper Nile, to be described below, is striking.[5]

In many parts of America we find myths strongly resembling those of Indonesia; the world is destroyed by a flood, and the sole survivors are a pair who are usually brother and sister; we also find slaughtered giants, dismembered corpses, and couples made from clay.

The Hareskin Indians say that all mankind, except the Wise Man, and his sister who was also his wife,

[1] Mothers, I, p. 366. [2] See note p. 197.
[3] H. G. Q. Wales, op. cit., pp. 68, 117. [4] Ibid., pp. 139 seq.
[5] See p. 159, and note p. 198.

were drowned in a great flood ; with the assistance of some animals he made a new world of mud.

The Haida Indians say that long ago all men and animals were destroyed in a flood, except a raven, whose mother was a woman who had no husband. The raven married a cockle, which produced a girl ; her he also married, and so became the ancestor of mankind. The raven also appears in the flood myth of the Loucheux Indians ; the sole survivor of the flood having killed the raven, repents, carefully collects and arranges its bones, and then reanimates it.

In the Kootenay (British Columbia) myth the wife of a hawk-man is ravished by a giant ; he shoots the giant in the breast with an arrow, in revenge for which the giant drinks up all the water. The wife plucks out the arrow from the giant's breast, whereupon the water gushes out and causes a flood, from which the pair take refuge on a mountain. In another version the giant is replaced by a fish, and the flood is caused by its blood.

The Mandans of the Plains observed an annual religious ceremony, and believed that if they did not perform it they would all be drowned by a flood. An incident of the ceremony was that a man pretended to be the sole survivor of a flood ; he was presented with knives, etc., which on the last day of the ceremony were thrown ritually into the river.

The Zunis of New Mexico say that they were once nearly exterminated by a flood, but threw a youth and maiden, dressed in their finest clothes, into the water, which at once began to subside. The youth and maiden were turned into stone. This turning of people into stone occurs in many Indonesian myths.

The Pima Indians of Colorado say that the 'Earth 'Doctor' made the world habitable by fashioning trees, mountains, etc., and finally moulded images of clay, which when he animated them became human beings. There being no death the world became overcrowded, so he pulled down the sky and crushed all living things to death, an unusual form of the myth which seems to echo Horace's 'Si fractus illabatur 'orbis . . .'[1] 'Earth Doctor' made a fresh start, but was superseded by 'Elder Brother'; the latter created a handsome youth, whom he caused to marry and have children by the Pima women. The period of gestation decreased till the youth became a husband and a father at the same time; this was apparently too much for 'Elder Brother', who proceeded to destroy the world by a flood. According to another Pima myth the world was re-peopled after the flood from mangled corpses found in an eagle's eyrie.

'According to a Mexican saga a dead man's bone, 'when sprinkled with blood, produced the father and 'mother of the present race of mankind'.[2]

The Chiriguanos of Bolivia say that once the whole tribe was drowned by a flood except a baby brother and sister, who were saved by floating on a large leaf till the water subsided; from their union the tribe is descended.

Crossing to Tahiti, we find that there all men are believed to be descended from a couple who were the sole survivors of a flood, a hurricane, and a rain of stones from the sky.

The Pelew Islanders say that the gods decided to destroy mankind by a flood, but warned an old woman

---

[1] *Odes*, III, 3.   [2] E. S. Hartland, op. cit., I, p. 74.

INCEST IN MYTH AND RITUAL

who had been kind to them to save herself by means of a raft. After the flood, when all mankind were drowned, they came to look for her, and found her dead on the raft, with her hair entangled in a tree. A goddess was instructed to enter her body and reanimate her, and she then became by the gods the mother of five children, who are the ancestors of mankind; the goddess then left her, and this time she died for good. The Akamba of East Africa tell a similar story.[1]

The Trobrianders have a myth in which, at the instigation of the sister, a brother and sister have intercourse in the sea. They retire to the shore, die clasped in each other's arms, and from their bodies grows the plant from which love charms are made.[2] We have here reminiscences of the images thrown into the water, the human sacrifice, the new world made from the victims' bones, and the ritual incest. Variants of the story occur in many European ballads,[3] while the fate of the lovers reminds us of the Bornean punishment for incest, by which the couple were taken to the river bank, and there impaled on a green bamboo stake, which was then allowed to grow.[4]

In New Zealand the creator made an exact copy of himself from red clay and his own blood, and animated it by blowing into its mouth and nostrils.

In Australia there are many such stories. The blacks of Victoria said that all mankind were destroyed by a flood except a man and a woman who climbed

---

[1] See note p. 198.
[2] B. Malinowski, op. cit., p. 126.
[3] For references see L. C. Wimberley, *Folklore in the English and Scottish Ballads*, p. 264; see also note p. 199.
[4] Hose and McDougall, op. cit., II, p. 196.

a tree on top of a high mountain. They also said that the creator made men by moulding them on pieces of bark which he cut with his sharp knife, and animated them by blowing into their mouths, noses, and navels.

From Africa a number of flood stories are reported, but since, in some cases at any rate, it seems doubtful whether they are not the result of missionary enterprise rather than genuine antiques, it is perhaps safer not to rely upon them. There are, however, undoubtedly genuine stories of how men emerged from rivers, or rivers from men, and water plays a very prominent part in African ritual. We also find stories of the incestuous origin of tribes. Thus Woto, cult-hero of the Bushongo, had by his sister a son, Nyimi Lele, who became founder of the Bashilele.[1] The leading rainmaker of the Transvaal is a woman called Majaji, who is alleged to be descended from a brother and sister, the children of a woman who killed her husband ritually.[2]

The Shiluk of the Upper Nile have a divine king who is killed when his strength begins to fail. Their creation myth is the story of the cult-hero Nyakang, who came from the land where there is no death. This land the Euhemerists seek higher up the Nile, though the cult, unknown in any area from which the Shiluk can be supposed to have migrated, has left abundant traces in the neighbourhood of Khartum. Nyakang and his companions came to a river choked with reeds, so slew a human victim, whose blood made a passage for them. Nyakang's son and daughter married and became the ancestors of the royal family,

---

[1] E. Torday, *On the Trail of the Bushongo*, p. 127.
[2] H. A. Stayt, *The Bavenda*, p. 312; see also note p. 199.

INCEST IN MYTH AND RITUAL

but the ordinary Shiluk are descended from various animals which Nyakang changed into men, and also from a couple who fell from heaven and were caught by him.[1] After the king is killed his body is left in a new house until it is completely decomposed; the bones are then placed in the centre of a canoe, and a boy and girl are tied one to each end of the canoe, which is then taken to the middle of the river and sunk.[2] We find a similar rite among the Kayans of Borneo: 'To the coffin (of a chief), which is shaped 'roughly like a boat, two small wooden figures are 'attached—a figure of a woman at the head, a male 'figure at its foot.'[3] I suggest that the king's remains represent those of last year's victim, and that the boy and girl (or the figures) represent last year's images.

Among the Azande of the Nile-Congo watershed clan exogamy is practised, and adultery is not taken very seriously. Chiefs, however, marry their sisters, and a man detected in adultery with the wife of a chief is, or was, tied to a tree and elaborately mutilated.[4] The victim, if he survives, bears no malice against the chief, which indicates that the proceeding is regarded as a rite, and I suggest that it goes back to a time when the chief himself ceased to be killed and cut up, but was replaced by a victim who had first to have ritual intercourse with the chief's sister-wife.

The tribes of Uganda practise clan exogamy; among the Baganda and Basoga the king or chief alone marries his sister, who becomes his queen or

---

[1] *Sudan Notes and Records*, I, p. 111.
[2] This is from my own Sudan notebook; Westermann's account, *The Shilluk* (sic) *People*, p. 136, is somewhat different.
[3] Hose and McDougall, op. cit., II, p. 34.
[4] *Sudan Notes and Records*, I, p. 258.

principal wife, but must on no account have children. Among the Banyoro, on the other hand, the king and princes marry their sisters and have children by them. The ordinary Baganda go through a marriage ceremony with their sisters, but really marry other women.

Among the Banyoro it was the custom in some cases to kill twins at birth, dry their bodies, keep them in the house for a year, and then throw them into a river or swamp. I conjecture that the cases in which this was done were those in which the twins were male and female, and that they were once identified with the images used in the creation rite. When twins are born in a Basoga clan, they are taken to the clan lands at sowing-time, and an elaborate ceremony is gone through to secure their good influence over the crops. Among the Baganda twins were always given male and female forms of the god's name; their parents received temporarily a divine or royal status, and went through a regular creation rite, which included a ritual pretence of intercourse in public, a ritual bathing in public, and the sacrifice of a goat.[1] I suggest that twins are everywhere regarded with veneration or horror according as they were once identified with the new or old images employed in the creation rite.

Actual brother-sister marriage is rare in other parts of Africa, but there are cases in which the king's sister acts as queen, though he does not marry her,[2] or where it is pretended that the chief's principal wife is his sister.[3] Similarly, we find that while in Peru, Bogota, and Hawaii the kings married their sisters,

[1] J. Roscoe, *The Baganda*, pp. 64, 84; *The Northern Bantu*, pp. 36, 48, 203, 235.   [2] R. S. Rattray, *Ashanti*, p. 81.
[3] H. A. Stayt, *The Bavenda*, p. 208.

in Samoa and Tonga the eldest sister of the king was treated as queen, though the king did not marry her.[1] To these facts I shall refer again later.

The last creation myths which we shall consider are those in the Book of Genesis. In Chapter xix we are told that God was angry with the cities of the plain, and destroyed them with fire and brimstone. The sole survivors are Lot and his family. His wife is killed and becomes a feature of the landscape; his daughters, because 'there is not a man in the earth 'to come in unto us', contrive to have intercourse with their father, and from the fruit of this intercourse two important tribes are descended. The fact that Lot and his daughters take refuge on a mountain-top suggests that a flood once formed part of the story; in other respects it conforms to type, though the substitution of two daughters for a sister or daughter is exceptional.

It seems to me possible, and indeed probable, that the story told in the earlier chapters is the same story,[2] but that the compilers, believing that it was a true story of how the world began, and not merely the description of a rite, suppressed certain incidents and altered the order of others. They suppressed the human sacrifice, because if Adam was the first man there could have been nobody to sacrifice, and put the flood after the creation because they did not see how the world could have been flooded before it was created. On the other hand it is possible that the story of Noah, like the story of Lot, was originally a separate version of the myth. At any rate the wording

[1] Mothers, III, p. 27.
[2] Mr. Hocart has already suggested (*Kingship*, p. 202) that the first chapter of Genesis is the account of a creation rite.

of Genesis i. 2 suggests that the world was in existence and covered with water before the creation, and Amos ix suggests that the Jews of an earlier day regarded the flood, the destruction of mankind, and the creation as recurrent rather than unique events. I shall later suggest that the story of Adam's rib is a vestige of the human sacrifice.

CHAPTER XXIII

THE CREATION RITE

WE are now in a position to suggest, in greater detail, what was actually done in the creation ritual. There are a great many features with which we are not immediately concerned, and which I have therefore left out of the stories. Such are the mock battle, in which it is essential that nobody shall be hurt; the procession of people disguised as animals ('the animals went in two by two'); the ritual use of obscene language by the women; the fire-altar (fire on a hilltop in the myths); the making of new fire; and the important part played by the snake. All these incidents are world-wide, or nearly so, and taken with those mentioned in the last chapter should suffice to convince any one who is not blinded by prejudice that all these myths and rites had a common origin. Confining ourselves, however, to the rites most nearly related to our problem, let us first consider where they took place. There can be little doubt that the sacred site was a tree on a mound or hill-top; not only do trees appear in many of the myths, but sacred trees are found all over the world; in some cases they are replaced by a maypole, and in others by a pillar. It seems that there was a circular trench round the tree, and outside it a fence to separate the ritual world from the real one. We now come to the flood, and its seems possible that it was composed of two elements; in the first place the last year's images and the remains of last year's victim were collected from the sacred enclosure, a ceremony was gone through to cause all the ills of the community to pass into them, and they were then thrown into the river. After this the youth and maiden who were to play the parts of king-brother and queen-sister appeared from the river, arriving probably by boat or raft; they were carried to the sacred enclosure, and made to climb into the sacred tree, in which there was perhaps a structure representing a boat. At this, or at an earlier stage, the sacred enclosure was drenched with water; this was to ensure an adequate supply for the ensuing year. In many of the South American myths which I have not quoted the flood was caused by the breaking of water-pots.

The next incident was the sacrifice of the human victim, the young man who had taken the part of the king-brother the previous year. His blood was caught in a bowl, and he was then dismembered. His skull and eyeballs were hung in the tree to represent the sky, sun, and moon; his larger bones were arranged round the outside of the circle to represent the mountains; such of his blood as was not required for other purposes was poured into the trench to represent the river or sea while other parts of his anatomy represented the animals and plants. Two ribs were set aside, as well as his skin, which had been carefully removed.

The next step was to take some clay, work it up into a suitable consistency with the victim's blood, and mould it on to the two ribs in the shape of a pair of human figures, male and female, which were then placed in the centre of the ' world '. The clay had probably to be obtained from the sacred site, and the youth and maiden to belong to the clan which owned that site, and which eventually became the royal clan. A ceremony of animating the figures was gone through, and the youth and maiden then came down from the tree, or ' descended from the sky '.

It would appear that the youth descended first, and that the girl had to look for and then make advances to him. Whether she pursued him round the enclosure, as in South Arabia, or was led round him, as at a Jewish wedding, is not clear. Possibly they represented the newly created sun and moon. It would appear, at any rate, that she, or both of them, ate the part of the human victim which was believed to contain his life-essence, probably the heart, that one of them put on his skin, and that they then had ritual intercourse.

This was the culminating point of the ritual, but whether it was followed by a general orgy, or whether the rite when fully performed replaced the orgy, is a question which I shall not attempt to answer here.

In discussing the sacrifice I assumed that it was the youth only who was killed, and most of the myths mention only a man or giant, the latter probably a later misunderstanding of the fact that mountains were made from his bones. Though the Egyptians, Greeks, and Mexicans sacrificed virgins on occasion, yet most of the rites included the sacrifice of a male victim only. The evidence suggests that originally the pair were both sacrificed at the end of the year, but that for some reason the practice of killing the queen-sister was abandoned much earlier than that of killing the king-brother, and that the sacrifice of the queen at the king's funeral, until recently the rule in India and Central Africa, was an indirect rather than a direct outcome of the creation rite.

When the queen-sister began to function for several

years in succession, she would have to renew her virginity annually, as Hera did in a stream near Argos,[1] and when the king-brother was also spared she would have to feign sisterhood, and to have or feign intercourse, with the man or animal that died in his stead.

All the foregoing is of course highly speculative, and many of the details may be wrong, but the general outline can hardly be so, since, as we have seen, it is confirmed by myths and rites from all parts of the world. All the evidence suggests that many thousands of years ago a magico-religious system, of which the central feature was a creation rite, was evolved in some centre of civilization, probably Egypt; that this creation rite spread all over the world, and that it is possible to reconstruct it from the creation myths and rites which have been recorded, or which are still in existence. The fact that this rite, which was evolved so long ago and has travelled so far, appears in almost the same form in every continent, is a striking testimony to the lack of originality in the human mind; such differences as exist appear to be due rather to variations in climate and fauna than to new ideas. We must also note that the reports upon which we have to rely have been made by people who did not realize the generally accepted connexion between floods, incest, and creation.

It is usual to 'explain' these rites by saying that the people are enacting a myth. Of course they are enacting a myth, but to say so explains neither the rite nor the myth. The rite, like all rites, is performed because people believe that their prosperity and the success of their undertakings depend on

[1] L. R. Farnell, op. cit., I, p. 218.

the performance, and they enact the myth because the myth tells them how to perform the rite properly; it is, as we have seen, the 'book of the words' of the rite, and it never was anything else.

The method adopted by the Euhemerists, in dealing with these myths, is to divide them up into a series of separate incidents, and to assume that these incidents are totally unconnected; they are then able to assume that the flood stories are traditions of a real flood; that the creation stories are the result of early speculation as to the origin of the universe, and that the incest stories are reminiscences of a practice of royal incest adopted from rational motives.

As regards the first, although we are not asked to believe in a universal deluge, yet we are to suppose that there are few if any parts of the world which were not at some time submerged by a flood, of which the sole survivors were a brother and sister.

The second theory is the result of a complete ignorance of savage mentality. In discussing the mythology of the Bantus, Lindblom [1] expresses astonishment at 'their great lack of feeling that the origin of the most 'important phenomena of existence needs explanation', but he need not be surprised, for there is no evidence that any savage has ever speculated about anything, or that in the days before Thales and Anaximenes any one took the slightest interest in the origin of the phenomena of existence. It is true that a mild scepticism has often been reported, but scepticism is not speculation, which is the prerogative of philosophers.[2]

The orthodox explanation of royal incest is that in

[1] Op. cit., p. 252.
[2] For a discussion of this question, see W. J. Perry, *The Children of the Sun*, pp. 476 seq.

ancient Egypt and elsewhere the succession went through the female line, so that the only way for a son to succeed his father was to marry his sister; but it obviously is not the only way—he could ignore the rule of succession. What justification is there for assuming that the law of succession was so sacred that nobody ever dared to challenge it, while the law of incest was so little regarded that ambitious and unscrupulous princes had no hesitation in breaking it? And what was the object of their ambition? Let us permit Sir James Frazer to tell us : ' At a certain stage ' of development the chief or king is rather the minister ' or servant of his people. The sacred functions which ' he is expected to discharge are deemed essential to ' the welfare, and even the existence, of the community, ' and at any cost some one must be found to perform ' them. Yet the burdens and restrictions of all sorts ' incidental to the early kingship are such that not ' merely in popular tales, but in actual practice, compulsion has sometimes been found necessary to fill ' vacancies, while elsewhere the lack of candidates ' has caused the office to fall into abeyance, or even to ' be abolished altogether. And where death stared ' the luckless monarch in the face at the end of a ' brief reign for a few months or days, we need not ' wonder that the gaols had to be swept and the dregs ' of society raked to find a king.' [1] We might suppose that the gaolbirds were the first to break the incest taboo, but that they would not be the queen's brothers.

Not only did kings in many lands marry their sisters, but, as we have seen, Egyptians of all classes habitually did so, and we are assured that this was

[1] GB, IV, p. 135.

done for a similar reason, namely, that they might acquire the property which belonged to their sisters by the Egyptian laws of inheritance. Yet Sir Gaston Maspero tells us that in the eyes of the Egyptians ' marriage between brother and sister was the best ' of marriages, and it acquired an ineffable degree of ' sanctity when the brother and sister who contracted ' it were themselves born of a brother and sister, who ' in their turn also sprang from a union of the same ' sort.'[1]

Among the Pueblo Indians of Arizona all land and houses belong to the women, who can divorce their husbands at will, yet they practise clan exogamy, and their incest laws are strict. We find a similar state of affairs in Assam and elsewhere.[2] The ancient Egyptians were the most religious people of whom we have any record, yet we are asked to believe that they, alone in the world, not merely condoned breaches of the incest taboo from motives of ambition and avarice, but actually canonized the breakers! That this view is held by some of the most eminent scientists of the day shows how little thought has really been devoted to these problems.

We know that sanctity in ancient Egypt was usually associated with the cult of the dead, and I shall later suggest that brother-sister marriage acquired its sanctity in this connexion.

---

[1] Quoted in GB, VI, p. 214. [2] Mothers, I, p. 300.

CHAPTER XXIV

THE HUSBAND AS BROTHER

AND the rib, which the Lord God had taken 'from man, made he a woman, and brought 'her unto the man. And Adam said, this is 'now bone of my bones, and flesh of my flesh. . . . 'Therefore shall a man leave his father and his mother 'and shall cleave unto his wife : and they shall be one 'flesh.'[1] We know that man does not lack a rib, and that a Jewish bridegroom, far from leaving his father and mother, brought his bride to live at their house, and we might be tempted to suppose that the passage is nonsensical. This would be a mistake, since words do not come to be regarded as inspired unless they mean something, even if it is not quite what the orthodox believe. In this case it seems to me that the words I have quoted, if properly understood, are not only true, but provide us with a valuable clue to the solution of our problem.

We saw in Chapter XXII that the story told in the early part of Genesis is, in all probability, a version of the universal creation myth, and comparing it with others, such as the Hindu account of how the yeoman was born from the side of the sacrificed man,[2] we may paraphrase the passage quoted above as follows : 'Since the first husband and wife, being made from 'the bones and blood of the same sacrificed man, were 'brother and sister, therefore shall every man leave 'his parental clan and join that of his wife, and they 'two shall be brother and sister.'

---

[1] Genesis ii. 22–24.   [2] A. M. Hocart, *Kingship*, p. 193.

THE HUSBAND AS BROTHER

We have seen that there arose, probably in Egypt, a creation ritual of which the central feature was the union of a brother and sister. In Egypt, owing to the development of a religious idea which we shall consider later, marriage between brother and sister became the rule in all classes, but in many countries there is brother-sister marriage in the royal family, while in many others there are myths of such unions, but no evidence that they actually took place. I suggest that in the former case the creation ritual was copied exactly, but when marriage began to spread beyond the royal family, the contest between the forces making for incest and those making for exogamy resulted in a compromise by which men did not really marry their sisters, but merely pretended to do so; in other words, they became their wives' brothers ritually at marriage.

In those cases in which there are incest myths but no record of incestuous marriages the same thing may have happened, except that it was the king, as well as the commoner, who pretended to marry his sister. We may suppose that in the countries most subject to Egyptian influence the idea of the husband as brother was strongest, and that the relationship tended to become symbolized as that influence became more remote.

We have seen kings marrying their sisters in many parts of the world, and also cases in which they pretend that their sisters are their wives or their wives their sisters; it is not only kings who have made this pretence. In the Book of Tobit,[1] Raguel says to Tobias: 'Take her, for thou art her cousin.' They are then married, after which Tobias says: 'And now, O

[1] Tobit, vii, 12.

'Lord, I take not this my sister for lust.' The wording suggests that by virtue of the marriage ceremony he had become her brother. In Uganda, on the other hand, we have seen that while kings married their sisters, less exalted persons went through a marriage ceremony with their sisters, but really married other women.[1] In other words, the Jew pretended that his wife was his sister, whereas the Baganda pretended that his sister was his wife.

A Bavenda bridegroom and bride actually become blood-brother and sister. 'The medicine-man . . . 'makes small incisions in the knees, hips, abdomens 'and necks of them both, and rubs the blood from the 'male into the female, and vice versa. . . . After 'the conclusion of this ceremony the two are husband 'and wife.'[2]

The theory that a man becomes his wife's brother explains a number of facts which seem otherwise inexplicable. It explains why a Christian may not marry his deceased wife's sister, and why Moslems and some other polygamists may not marry two sisters at the same time. It may explain another strange Moslem law, that a man who has divorced his wife by the threefold divorce cannot marry her again until she has been married and divorced by another man. It is possible that the brother relationship to his former wife remains after the divorce, and can only be broken by her marrying another.

An Orthodox priest must be married, but if his wife dies must not marry again. Why is this? I suggest that in pre-Christian times the priesthood descended

[1] J. Roscoe, *The Baganda*, p. 122.
[2] H. A. Stayt, *The Bavenda*, p. 149; see also notes pp. 199 and 200.

in the female line, and a man therefore acquired his priesthood in virtue of his wife. If, then, his wife died, he could not marry her sister, because she had become his sister, nor could he marry another woman, because he would become her brother, and so lose his title to the priesthood. Similarly in Samoa, if a chief wishes to marry again he must lay aside his rank and pretend to be a youth.[1] The idea seems to be that if a chief married again he would lose his chieftainship. At Rome the Flamen Dialis lost his priesthood if his wife died.

There are many reasons for believing that group exogamy was once universal, but if so its disappearance from the Mediterranean area has never been explained. The system depends on permanence of status, and once men began to change their status by becoming their wives' brothers, a confusion would ensue which would inevitably lead to the breakdown of the system. Clan exogamy might continue to exist in theory after it had ceased to exist in fact, and it is possible that the squabbles of medieval theologians as to what were the prohibited degrees were really attempts to combine the system of bilateral kinship with the clan exogamy of the Nordic tribes, and that Luther was unjust to the Popes when he accused them of prohibiting certain forms of cousin marriage in order to make money by granting dispensations. The minds of priests are rooted in the past, and though they often exploit old dogmas, they seldom, if ever, invent new ones. And this brings us to our next point.

There are many cases in which marriages which would otherwise be unlawful become lawful, or in

[1] Margaret Mead, *Coming of Age in Samoa*, p. 191.

which 'the guilt of incest can be atoned', by a ritual of which the central feature is a blood sacrifice. Among the Wahehe of East Africa cross-cousins may marry, but the marriage will be unfruitful unless the bride's father sacrifices a sheep.[1] In Madagascar the marriage of cross-cousins, or of the children of two brothers, is permitted, but only if there is a sacrifice, and the parties are sprinkled with blood. Among the Kikuyu of East Africa the marriage of first and second cousins is prohibited, but should such a marriage be contracted unknowingly, the dreadful consequences can be averted by placing a sheep on the woman's shoulders, and slaughtering it in such a way that she is bathed in its blood. Similarly in Northern Celebes marriages between cousins are not allowed, but may be atoned for by the sacrifice of a goat. Among the Sea Dayaks of Borneo the goat is replaced by a pig; this is to prevent the rice from being blasted. ' In both islands 'the idea seems to be that the marriage of first cousins 'is a crime which, either in itself, or through the divine 'wrath it excites, threatens to blight all the fruits of 'the earth, and that fertility can only be restored to 'the ground by libations of blood, particularly of pig's 'blood, which, in the opinion of not a few peoples, 'possesses a singular efficacy for the atonement of 'moral guilt, particularly the guilt of incest.'[2]

Sir James seems to have realized that among most of the more primitive peoples those who have committed incest either are killed themselves or must die by deputy in the shape of whatever animal is regarded as the proper substitute; and that failure to adopt

[1] For this and the following examples see FOT, II, pp. 156 seq.
[2] Ibid., p. 173.

this procedure leads to failure of the crops. The religious term 'moral guilt' is, however, quite inapplicable to the magical attitude of mind which he describes. In some parts of India it is still considered impious to rescue people who have been seized by the sacred crocodiles; in other parts of the world people who fall into the water are left to drown, or even thrust back in. Why is this? Because they have performed the first part of a rite of human sacrifice, and to rescue them is not merely to deny the powers that be their due, but to snatch it from them when they have already received it. Floods, or other calamities, are bound to follow such conduct. In the same way, as we have seen, those who perform the ritual incest in the creation rite become the victims destined for sacrifice, and therefore those who commit incest have performed the first part of a rite of human sacrifice, and have become victims dedicated to the powers. Failure to consummate this dedication is, in the opinion of the savage, naturally followed by the most appalling calamities, and since one of the chief objects of the creation rite is to assure the food supply, famine is only too probable. The savage causes those who have committed incest to be sacrificed or to sacrifice, not because he believes that it will atone for moral guilt, but because it will complete the rite, and thereby rescue him from the danger of starvation.

But just as in many parts of the world we find blood-money replacing blood-revenge, so we find a payment replacing the blood-sacrifice. A Masai of East Africa who marries his cousin presents her father with a cow,[1]

---

[1] Ibid., p. 165. Sir James conjectures that the cow is killed, but his authority does not say so.

and in similar circumstances a Mohave of California presents his father-in-law with a horse.[1] A Roman Catholic averts the dangers of incest by paying a sum of money to the Pope, and receiving a dispensation, presumably from the blood-sacrifice.

The blood-sacrifice is sometimes explained as ' killing ' the relationship ', but that this is merely a rationalization seems clear from the fact that the sacrifice and partition of a victim is practised all over the world as a rite of communion or alliance,[2] and that rites similar to those which among some East African tribes are alleged to kill the relationship are practised by other tribes of the same area to cure barrenness where there is no question of relationship at all.[3]

I have already suggested that in the original creation rite the brother and sister partook of that part of the victim, probably his heart, which was supposed to contain his life-essence. It would seem that this is an important part of the marriage rite, and is therefore practised by those who think that their union is not blessed, whether on the ground of relationship or not. In the ordinary way the life-essence may be conveyed by a substitute for the blood-sacrifice, a cake cut in half, or a bowl of porridge shared, a pretended sacrifice made by a pretended brother and sister; but where there is a possibility that the relationship may be real, then the sacrifice must also be real, and where the woman's barrenness shows that the life-essence has not been transmitted, there, again, there must be a blood-sacrifice. It would seem then that the slaughtered animal plays two parts: it represents the human

---

[1] A. L. Kroeber, op. cit., p. 747. [2] FOT, I, 392, seq.
[3] J. Roscoe, *The Baganda*, p. 46; *The Northern Bantup*, p. 42.

victim at the creation rite, and thereby provides the necessary life-essence, and it represents the brother and sister themselves, and thereby absolves them from being sacrificed at the next rite.

We have still another custom to consider: why, in the Trobriand Islands and elsewhere, though the young people of both sexes are allowed the utmost liberty in their sexual relations, must brothers and sisters avoid each other? That is to say, why must they never play together, and if they have occasion to speak, only do so in the most formal manner? We have seen reason to believe that in the creation rite the images which represented the first man and woman were made afresh each year, and that in the myths the young man and woman who are represented as coming down from heaven or being the sole survivors on earth are generally assumed to be virgins, and we may well suppose that the young couple who were, or were supposed to be, brother and sister, and who performed the act of ritual intercourse at the rite, had to be virgins. If, then, there were communities in which every one had complete sexual liberty, within the limits of the law of exogamy, except those pairs of brothers and sisters who were destined to play the principal parts in the creation rite, precautions would have to be taken to preserve their virginity, and these precautions would have special reference to their relations with each other, since the rest of the young people would be afraid to meddle with the sacred beings. The ritual of incest and human sacrifice tended in most places to become gradually symbolized, and eventually the human actors ceased to play their parts, but the agelong tradition remained, and brothers and sisters must still avoid each other. This view receives some confirmation from what Professor Malinowski[1] tells us of the Malasi clan, who are the ruling clan in the Trobriands, and in former times may well have had to produce the royal victims. He tells us that though brother-sister incest is regarded with horror, it nevertheless occurs, and is especially prevalent in this clan, to which belonged the hero and heroine of the incest myth related above.[2]

In some places, such as Uganda, avoidance is between cross-cousins, and it is possible that when the creation rite reached those parts the impact of the new beliefs was not at first strong enough to impose actual brother-sister union, and that cross-cousins, the nearest relatives whose union was sanctioned by the law of exogamy, were made to play the parts of brother and sister.

We have seen reason to believe that the original marriage was a ritual union of a king-brother and a queen-sister in the creation rite. They were united until death parted them, which it did not long afterwards. Besides the evidence already adduced there is the fact that in many parts of the world bridegroom and bride are treated as king and queen; in the Russian rite, to take a well-known example, royal crowns are held over their heads.[3] Why this marriage rite continued to be performed by royalties even after human sacrifice had been abolished and even when, in many cases, they no longer married their sisters, is clear. They were still responsible for the weather and the crops, and had therefore still to perform a creation rite, though its form had become modified. But how

[1] Op. cit., p. 97. [2] p. 157. [3] A. M. Hocart, *Kingship*, pp. 99 seq.

did commoners come to perform this rite? Imitation, after the origin and purpose of the rite had been forgotten, may account for the fact, but only if a belief had arisen that the rite conferred some benefit on the king, a benefit which could also be conferred on the commoner. It came to be believed, if I am correct, that the marriage rite made the king a father, and we shall have to consider what a father is, and why a man should wish to become one.

CHAPTER XXV

WHAT IS A FATHER?

THE obvious answer to this question is, as is often the case, the wrong one; the root word from which the word for father in all the Aryan languages is derived appears to mean nothing but 'owner', and the same applies to the Semitic *ab, abu*. How has it come about that a word which meant 'owner' now means 'begetter'? The answer is that it has not; the word 'father' has no necessary connexion with begetting. When we are told that Mr. So-and-so is the father of the House of Commons, it never occurs to us to suppose that all the other members are his offspring; what we understand is that the fact that he has been there the longest is thought to give him a larger stake in the place, to make him in a sense its owner.

The word 'father', or its equivalent in other languages, is most commonly used in the sense of the owner of children, but when we try to find out what it is that makes a man the owner of children we learn that the fact that he has or has not begotten them has little or nothing to do with it. He is their owner or father because he has performed a magical rite which is believed, explicitly or implicitly, to have transferred to them a portion of what may be called his life-essence. This rite makes him their father whether he has begotten them or not.

The Dieri, a tribe of Central Australia, are ignorant of physiological paternity, but 'though the father is a 'social and spiritual parent rather than one by blood, 'yet some affinity to the father, akin to the blood bond, 'is felt to exist.'[1]

The Ashanti social system is based upon the belief that children are composed of blood, which is derived from the mother, and 'spirit', which is derived from the father.[2] Many savages have similar beliefs, and I suggest that this spirit is what I have called 'life-essence', and is transmitted magically from the bridegroom to the bride at the marriage rite.

Among the Romans the only people who were called *patres*, patricians, or fathers were the nobles, and they were the only people who went through a regular marriage rite, which included dividing and eating a wedding cake, and sitting together on a skin of a sacrificed sheep. By this means, I suggest, they imparted life-essence to their wives, and thereby became the fathers of children bearing their names, while the children of plebeians were nameless and fatherless. Another point to be noted is that a Roman nobleman was thought to be more closely related to his adopted than to his begotten son. The former took all his adopted father's names, and with them no doubt a goodly portion of his life-essence. It seems possible that the practice of adopting children may have originated in a belief that adopted children receive a double dose of life-essence.

The Todas of Southern India are apparently aware of the fact of physiological paternity, yet when a woman reaches the seventh month of pregnancy she goes into the forest with her husband, or one of her husbands,

---

[1] A. P. Elkin, JRAI, 1931, p. 497.
[2] R. S. Rattray, *Ashanti*, p. 46.

for the Todas are polyandrous, and an elaborate ceremony is gone through, in the course of which the man makes a miniature bow and arrow, and names it with his clan name, and the woman places it against her forehead. After this he cooks a ritual meal, which they eat together. 'The ceremony is of the greatest 'importance from the social point of view, and the 'fatherhood of the child depends entirely upon it. 'The man who gives the bow and arrow is the father 'of the child for all social purposes, and is regarded 'as such even if he has had nothing to do with the 'woman before the ceremony. The ceremony must 'always be performed during the first pregnancy of a 'woman, and it takes place in any succeeding preg-'nancy only when it is desired for any reason to alter 'the fatherhood of the children. One of the most serious 'scandals in Toda society is the birth of a child when 'the mother has not been through this ceremony.'[1] I suggest that the man confers life-essence upon the woman by means of the bow, the name, and the ritual meal.

Our English law is very similar to that of the Todas. If a man marries a woman whom he has never seen before, and she gives birth to a child on the following day, he is its father. If a man is sexually impotent, he can still marry and have lawful children. I know of a case in which a married woman had intercourse with a negro, and gave birth to a black child; it is the husband, and not the negro, who is its father. On the other hand, a man who begets an illegitimate child may have to pay for it, but he does not give it his name, and has no paternal rights over it; in other

[1] W. H. R. Rivers, *The Todas*, p. 322.

WHAT IS A FATHER ?

words, he is the recognized begetter, but not the sociological father. That these are not merely questions of law is shown by the beliefs that a child gets its body from its mother, and its mind from its father, which is almost as widespread in England as in Ashanti, and that all a woman's children resemble her first husband. This latter superstition has been extended to animals, and a hundred years ago was solemnly discussed by the Royal Society. When a man marries a pregnant woman, he makes, in popular parlance, ' an ' honest woman of her '. An honest woman is one, it would seem, who by means of the marriage rite and the transfer of name is able to confer life-essence upon her child, which would otherwise be illegitimate, and therefore, in popular belief, deficient in vitality.[1] This being the case, it becomes clear why bastards, other than royal bastards, are almost everywhere despised and disapproved of, and why among so many savage races unmarried girls are allowed the fullest licence, yet are compelled to resort to abortion if they become pregnant.

The theory that the bridegroom confers upon his bride by means of the marriage rite an inexhaustible supply of life-essence explains how it is that children can be recognized as the legitimate offspring of men who died, two, three, or even ten years before they were born, as according to Mrs. Hasluck,[2] has happened in Albania during the present century; it also explains how the Jews, and many modern savages,[3] could raise up seed to their deceased brother by having intercourse with his widow, and why, if an Akamba

---

[1] A. S. E. Ackerman, *Popular Fallacies*, p. 415.
[2] *Man*, 1932, 65.   [3] Mothers, I, p. 777.

marries his brother's widow and has children by her, they call him ' uncle '.[1] The idea seems to be that the life-essence is there, but requires stimulation.

Mr. Briffault says:[2] ' It is sometimes said that the ' purpose of marriage is the procreation of children ; ' but it is evident that marriage is not necessary to ' achieve that object, and it cannot therefore have arisen ' to fulfil a purpose for which it is not required.' This argument is fallacious. In the first place, because while it is evident to us that the rainfall does not depend on the activities of a rainmaker, it is not evident to the savage. In the second place, while the facts of procreation may be evident to the biologist, they are by no means evident to the layman, and before the seventeenth century, when scientific investigation into the subject was initiated by William Harvey, the fact that pregnancy is due to sexual intercourse could have been no more than an inference from observed coincidences. It is obvious, then, that people who used the word ' procreation ' three hundred years ago could not possibly have meant by it what Mr. Briffault means. It is very doubtful whether gametes have yet penetrated to those misty heights upon which theologians discuss questions of sexual morality, and it is quite possible that what procreation, or its equivalent in other languages, originally meant, was not causing children to be born, but to be born properly supplied with life-essence.

It is widely believed that life-essence is indestructible, and that the quantity of spirit, or number of souls, or however one may choose to express it, in a community is limited, so that the number of births balances the

[1] G. Lindblom, op. cit., p. 85. [2] Mothers, I, p. 520.

number of deaths. This belief survives among some who are not savages, and I was assured by the Moslem peasants of Transjordan that the number of Samaritans at Nablus had always been the same, and that births and deaths took place simultaneously. I think sixty-six was the number they gave me, though in fact there were about one hundred and fifty. It is possible that the Nasamonian custom is connected with this belief; the custom is so called because it was reported by Herodotus[1] of the Nasamones of Cyrenaica, and it was also reported by Diodorus of the inhabitants of the Balearic Islands. In modern times it has been stated to occur in various parts of East Africa, Australia, the Pacific Islands, Central and South America, and the West Indies, while traces of its former existence have been found in India, China, France, and Ireland.[2] The custom consists in all the male guests at a wedding having intercourse with the bride. It has been explained as a ransom which a man pays to his clan brothers for his right to an individual wife, but this explanation is put out of court by the fact that the bride's own relatives, whom she could not marry, are among those who have intercourse with her.[3] It seems that we must place the rite, on the one hand, with those cases in which a girl is ritually deflowered by her father or some other relative, and on the other with the orgies which take place at harvest festivals, or similar ceremonies, at which the laws of incest are suspended. It is clear that even where incest is most dreaded acts of incest are regarded as sometimes necessary, and the reason may be that the life-essence of the clan is believed to be vested in the men of the

---

[1] IV, 172. [2] Mothers, III, pp. 223-6. [3] Ibid., p. 318.

clan, and to be passed on by them to the women of the clan. At any rate there can be little doubt that these customs are connected with the ideas which made an act of ritual incest the central feature of the creation rite.

Now marriage is not the mere cohabitation of a man and a woman, but a ritual union, and fatherhood, as we have seen, is not the mere begetting of children, but is a result of such union. This ritual union could only come into existence owing to a belief that it would confer some benefit upon the parties; and though, as we have seen, all the evidence suggests that it was a modified imitation of the creation rite, it could obviously not have been an imitation of that rite in its original form, since in that form the couple who were married were destined for sacrifice. The commoner would only wish to imitate the king when the lot of the king had become enviable, and when it had come to be believed that a benefit was conferred upon the king by the creation rite which could be conferred upon the commoner by a similar rite. I have already suggested that this benefit was fatherhood, but why should a man wish to be a father? Those who hope to solve these problems by gazing earnestly into the fire instead of studying the facts will no doubt answer, 'the paternal instinct', but why can this 'instinct' only be satisfied by a son, never by daughters, and why in so many civilized communities is a man who has no son considered to be in a parlous state? Why must one invent an imaginary son when addressing a sonless Arab, and why in the mind of a Hindu are the ideas of paternity and immortality so closely connected? The last part of the question suggests the answer: a man is immortal only if he has a son. This belief has become modified both in language and ideas, but is still general, even among ourselves; a man wishes for a son to bury him and look after his grave; to keep his memory green; to succeed to his name or his title, and so keep it alive; to keep up the old place and the old family portraits. The Roman nobles kept their ancestors alive by means of portrait statues, and these bring us back to Egypt, and the portrait statues which were associated with mummification. The whole question is far too large and complex to be adequately dealt with here, and all I shall do is to suggest a possible connexion between ritual incest, fatherhood, and immortality.

A very important landmark in the history of the kingship was when the king, as he had now become, ceased to be killed at the end of the year, but was given an extended tenure of office, a tenure which tended to become longer and longer, till in most cases it eventually coincided with the term of his natural life. How this change came about it seems at present impossible even to guess, but come about it undoubtedly did. In many parts of the world another man died in the king's stead,[1] but in Egypt the evidence seems to suggest that the representative of the king was the bull, which later became a god under the name of Apis. Now, while the flesh and blood of a bull might be an adequate substitute for human flesh and blood, the bones of the bull, and especially its skull, would be very different from human bones, and the custom might arise of keeping the bones of the last sacrificed king, and using them for several years in succession. The

[1] For a discussion on these questions see GB, IV, 'The Dying God'.

obvious way to do this would be to collect them from round the sacred enclosure, and arrange them in such a way that with the assistance of the bull's blood they looked as much as possible like the remains of a newly slaughtered man. The more realistic the remains could be made to look the less would be the necessity for a fresh victim, so that the new king, if he wished for a long reign, would have every inducement to preserve the remains of his predecessor as carefully as possible. Eventually the time would come, as it did come, when the king was succeeded by his son by the sister-bride with whom he had gone through the creation ceremonies, and by this time it would have become the son's duty to preserve the remains of his father, and so immortalize him. Eventually the long succession of dead and immortalized kings became amalgamated into one dead and immortalized king, Osiris, the dead god and god of the dead. It has been suggested that Osiris was a real king, the founder of Egyptian civilization ; if a succession of live kings can give rise to the idea of a live god, a succession of dead kings may well give rise to the idea of a dead god, but there seems to be no more reason why Rameses II should become the real dead king Osiris than why Henry VIII should become William the Conqueror. Eventually the belief arose that commoners as well as kings could become Osiris if they observed the proper ritual. This consisted in going through the creation rite, or a modified form of it, with their sisters, and thereby conferring life-essence, and with it health and prosperity, upon their sons, who in their turn mummified their fathers, and thereby immortalized them. This explains the sanctity of brother-sister marriages. When these ideas penetrated beyond Egypt, the extent to which they were put into operation depended on the extent to which the desire for personal immortality was able to overcome the fear of breaking the law of exogamy. We have seen what happened in Palestine and Uganda; in Greece the problem was solved by causing every bridegroom and bride to represent Zeus the brother-god, and Hera the sister-goddess.[1] This explanation may seem far-fetched, and so perhaps it is, but the explanations which have previously been put forward seem to me to be no less far-fetched in themselves, while in addition they are difficult, if not impossible, to reconcile with one another.

There have been many variations and developments of these ideas, which it is tempting but perhaps unnecessary to deal with here, but which have confused our own ideas of paternity to such an extent that most Englishmen have at least five fathers. There is the Heavenly Father, who confers immortality upon us at baptism by means of the priest, the Father in God; unbaptized babes have no souls. There is the King, the father of his people, to whom we send our daughters dressed as brides, that he may confer life-essence upon them; in the opinion of many old ladies this rite lost its efficacy when during his recent illness his place was taken by the Queen. Then there is our godfather, who confers upon us his name, and with it no doubt a portion of his life-essence; and finally there are our father-in-law and our mother's husband.

There is one more problem which has some bearing on our theme, and which it would be cowardly to shirk, the problem of the couvade. The custom of

[1] L. R. Farnell, op. cit., I, p. 192.

couvade consists in a man being put to bed when his wife has a baby. His treatment while there has varied greatly, for while among the Caribs of the West Indies he was starved and tortured, in the Moluccas of the East Indies he was given every luxury. In the more modified forms of the rite, in California, Borneo, or the Sudan, he has merely to observe certain food or other taboos, while in England he is believed to suffer from certain ailments, especially toothache.

We have seen that in the creation rite two men were concerned, the man who was sacrificed and the man who was married, and the evidence suggests that the girl who was married was believed to obtain life-essence from both of them. In time the human victim was abolished, or replaced by an animal, and it seems possible that doubts then arose as to whether the life essence was being properly transmitted, and that a pretence was made of killing the husband, extracting life-essence from him, and then restoring him to life. There is no doubt that in some cases the custom is definitely connected with the transfer of life-essence; among the Ainu of Japan, ' as soon as the child was ' born the father had to consider himself very ill, and ' had therefore to stay at home wrapped by the fire. ' . . . The idea seems to have been that life was passing ' from the father into his child.'[1] In Eastern India, where the custom is widely observed, it was explained to one investigator that ' the life had gone out of the ' man '.[2] Couvade, it would seem, is part of the price which the father in magic pays for immortality.

[1] Quoted by Mr. Warren R. Dawson on p. 27 of his *Custom of Couvade*, where the whole subject is fully discussed.
[2] Quoted by Mr. A. M. Hocart, *Man*, 1931, 281.

CHAPTER XXVI

OEDIPUS AND JOCASTA

I HAVE now completed the task which I set myself, that is, to furnish an explanation of the incest taboo in the many inconsistent and even contradictory forms in which we find it, and I have suggested that all these differences are the result of compromises, in varying degrees, between a very ancient magical belief that it is dangerous to have intercourse with a woman who lives on the same side of the stream, and a newer, but still ancient, religious belief that in order to ensure his survival after death a man must marry his sister.

That I have proved these theories I do not for a moment suggest. The first is nothing more than what seems to be a plausible guess, which differs from previous guesses in that it takes into account such evidence as there is, and attempts to cover all the facts which have to be explained. The second theory has a good deal more evidence to support it; and though I do not venture to suggest that it is the complete explanation, yet I believe that when that has been arrived at it will prove to include the processes which I have outlined here. That the complete explanation will be found I have no doubt, but it will not be until it is more generally realized that the way to gain a knowledge of human origins is to examine, sift, and compare the evidence, and that we shall get no further by trying to imagine how a stockbroker would act if turned loose in the primeval forest without his clothes.

There is one other point to be noted, and that is that the rites with which I have dealt, whether I have explained them correctly or not, must have taken an immensely long period of time to be evolved. That the creation rite began as a rite of human sacrifice is most unlikely; things do not begin as suddenly as that. Perhaps at first all shed a few drops of blood, and later a finger-joint, until at the end probably of thousands of years one person was chosen by lot to give his or her blood for the community. No doubt it took many more millennia to evolve the idea of a royal clan, the members of which received certain privileges in consideration of living and dying for the community, and even then the idea of a divine and omnipotent king was still very far off. Humanity is very slow to learn and very slow to forget, and traces of the most primitive of these ideas survive to this day, not merely among savages, but even among ourselves.

I have one task left, and that is to return to the Oedipus myth, and consider it in the light of the facts which I have adduced in this book, and particularly in Chapters XXI and XXII. Is it really a myth, or is it a true story? Dr. Farnell[1] assures us that it is ' a great and terrible story preserved by tradition ' of ' a mortal king of tragic history ', but does he believe in the Sphinx? If not, what justification has he for accepting the story yet rejecting some of its principal incidents? If I say, ' I do not believe that there was ' a real person called Peter Pan,' I am, historically speaking, correct; yet my small daughter would be quite justified in saying that there was a person called Peter Pan, and that he flew in through the window,

[1] *Greek Hero Cults*, p. 334.

because she did see a person who was called Peter Pan, and that person did fly in through the window. But what Dr. Farnell and his school say amounts to this, ' We firmly believe that there was a person called ' Peter Pan, but we do not believe that he flew in ' through the window. No doubt he really walked up ' the stairs.'

Let us consider the story of Oedipus. The son of a king and queen, he is condemned to death at birth ; so were Perseus and Jason. He is brought up by the king of a foreign country ; so were Perseus and Theseus. He causes his father's death ; so did Perseus and Theseus. He overcomes a monster and becomes king, but is subsequently dethroned ; the same fate befell Theseus and Bellerophon. Finally he disappears from a hilltop ; so did Theseus and Heracles. Similar incidents occur in the stories of Romulus, Moses, and many other cult-heroes in various parts of the world, and there can be little doubt that these stories are variants of the same myth, that is to say, they are accounts of a ritual which was performed, with slight variations, over a wide area.

If we pull aside the magnificent though sombre cloak which has been thrown over Oedipus by the great tragedians, we find a lay figure which differs from a large number of other such figures, of which but a few have been mentioned above, in two features only ; he marries his mother, and he loses his eyes. The latter feature is, I suggest, a vestige of a rite which has been already noticed many times, the rite in which the eyeballs of the divine victim were hung from the sacred tree to represent the sun and moon ; his marriage to his mother requires further investigation.

We have seen reason to believe that in the original creation rite, after it had become fully developed, the divine king was killed annually, but that the period of his life and reign was, in most countries, gradually extended. Sometimes he reigned till a man, who became his successor, managed to kill him; sometimes till his strength began to fail, and sometimes for a fixed term of years. Sir James Frazer has adduced much evidence to suggest that in ancient Greece the term of a king's reign was fixed at eight years,[1] and it seems probable that the period during which this system obtained coincided with the period in which the myths referred to above, including the Oedipus myth, took their shape. Now if this is the case, one fact is obvious, that a king can seldom, if ever, have been succeeded by his son, or his son-in-law. The heroes are usually, if not invariably, represented as succeeding their fathers or fathers-in-law while still in the first flush of youth; but apart from this it is clear that unless men become fathers at the age of eight, they cannot normally be succeeded by their adult children at the end of an eight years' reign.

I have suggested that the practice of killing the queen-sister as well as the king-brother once formed part of the creation ritual, but that at a very early stage the practice of killing the queen-sister was abandoned, and that the new king married the queen, and became ritually her brother. In Egypt and Persia, as we have seen, kings often married their mothers as well as their sisters, but it is very doubtful if this practice really spread to Europe. The explanation I suggest of the Oedipus myth is as follows: so long as the tenure

[1] GB, IV, pp. 58 seq.

of the kingship was octennial a king could not be succeeded by his son, but was succeeded by a foreign prince. This prince had to kill him, and then by drinking his blood, or performing some such rite, and possibly also by performing his obsequies, became his son. He also married the queen, and thereby became her brother, and since he was ritually the son of her late husband, her son also. The myth, as usual, was modified more slowly than the rite, and stories of how princes had been spirited away to some foreign country immediately after birth were invented to explain how Oedipus, for example, was the son of the king of Thebes and the reputed son of the king of Corinth. He, or rather the line of kings whom he typifies, was really the son of the king who reared him, and only ritually the son of the king whom he succeeded.

If the queen was no longer young, the new king would probably be married to a princess, and would become her brother but not her son. Perhaps this fact is enshrined in such myths as that of Macareus, and it is to be noted that Creon, who brings about the downfall of Oedipus and becomes his successor, is Jocasta's brother.

It came about gradually, according to Sir James, that instead of being killed at the end of eight years, the king merely died by deputy or went through a rite of some other description, and then obtained another eight years' lease of life and office. Two results would ensue: in the first place the old queen would be an old woman, and would therefore not be married to the new king; and in the second place the king's own son would be available to succeed him. Thus while the myth of the king's blood-relationship to the queen would tend to be symbolized or to die out, since it had never been a fact, the myth of the new king's blood-relationship to the old king would become a fact, and would give rise to the principle of hereditary kingship in the male line.

In the rest of Greece the tradition of royal incest either died out or merely survived in certain vague myths of the gods, or in the incomplete stories of Macareus and Thyestis. It is the myth of Oedipus which, if taken in conjunction with the other facts which have been set forth in this book, supplies us with the solution to a puzzling mythological problem —which, in fact, enables us to guess the riddle of the Sphinx.[1]

---

[1] See note, p. 200

NOTES

P. 15. **Ignorance of physiological paternity.**

Since the appearance of Professor Malinowski's paper, doubts have been expressed as to whether this ignorance is anywhere so extensive as he asserts, and Mr. A. G. Rentoul denies that in the Trobriand Islands it exists at all.[1]

P. 99. '**There appears to be no word for incest in any savage language.**'

I have since found an exception in the Lambas, who call incest *ishiku*. Among them incest with a sister is apparently less serious than with a sister's daughter or a maternal uncle's wife.[2]

P. 127. **Men crossing water to women.**

The Krachi say that the god Wulbari sent men down on one side, and women on the other, of the River Frao. After a time the men tired of celibacy, and crossed to the women.[3]

P. 154. **Izanagi and Izanami.**

The earliest extant Japanese myths are contained in the Kojiki, which is, according to the translator,[4] a not very successful attempt to combine three legendary cycles, emanating originally from three different provinces. Much of it is confused, but we can nevertheless pick out a number of familiar features. The ocean ('brine') was in existence before the work of creation began.[5] When

[1] MAN, 1932, 325.
[2] C. M. Doke, *The Lambas of Nothern Rhodesia*, pp. 70–1.
[3] A. W. Cardinall, *Tales Told in Togoland*, p. 230.
[4] B. H. Chamberlain, *The Kojiki*, pp. lxxxv. seq.
[5] p. 19.

Izanagi and Izanami meet round the pillar, it is the sister who accosts the brother; their first child is placed in a boat of reeds, after which they proceed with the work of creation.[1] Izanagi beheads his youngest son, from whose limbs the mountain gods are made.[2] The sun-goddess and moon-god are born from Izanagi's eyes.[3] Another son, Susa-no-Wo, after a curious intrigue and quarrel with his sister, has his finger- and toe-nails pulled out by the other gods and is expelled from heaven. Later, after killing a huge serpent, and marrying the maiden whom it was about to devour, he reappears as god of Hades.[4] His son, or descendant, Oho-na-Muji, is killed by the eighty deities, who crush him in a tree. Being restored to life, he visits his father, or ancestor, in the other world, and marries, his sister, or great-great-aunt, the Forward Princess, so called because she does the courting. Returning to earth with her after various ordeals, he drowns the eighty deities in rivers, and 'then he began to make the land'. In other words, he performs a creation rite.[5]

P. 154. **Boat burial.**

Among the Lambas the body of a chief is left on a platform until it has decomposed. The bones are then placed in a canoe, which is carried to the burial-place slung on a specially made pole.[6]

P. 157. **Akamba flood myth.**

A village once stood where there is now a sheet of muddy water. One wet evening a frog came hopping into one of the huts. Among the Akamba this is an evil omen, and the children drove it out. It tried other huts, till at last a mother told her children to let it warm itself by the fire. After warming itself the frog told the woman to

---
[1] p. 21.   [2] p. 36.   [3] p. 46,   [4] pp. 52, seq.
[5] pp. 84-88. See also W. G. Aston, *Shinto*, pp. 21-8.
[6] C. M. Doke, op. cit., pp. 186-8.

take her children, and as much of her goods as she could carry, and leave the village at once. 'I shall destroy the others for their unkindness,' it said; 'I am a spirit.' Hardly had she got outside the village when she heard a great rush of water; the village was submerged, and all the inhabitants drowned.[1]

P. 157. **An Icelandic incest myth.**

In Iceland the mountain-ash is regarded as sacred. A story localized in two places tells how a brother and sister were accused of incest and executed in spite of their denials. They were buried on either side of the church and two mountain-ash trees, springing one from each grave, interlaced their branches over the roof. This was regarded as a sign of their innocence.[2] In an English variant, however, the pair are not brother and sister, but luckless lovers, and the branches twine themselves into a 'true-lovers' knot.'

P. 158. **Incest myths in Africa.**

The Anuak of the Sudan-Abyssinian frontier claim descent from a brother and sister, the children of a brother and sister,[3]

It appears to be believed that Chimpipi, cult-hero of the Lambas, married his sister and by her had a son who sacrificed him, and who is the reputed ancestor of the Lamba chiefs.[4]

P. 172. **The husband as brother in Japan.**

The translator of the Kojiki tells us that in that work 'the wife is constantly spoken of as *imo*, i.e., "younger "sister". In fact sister and wife were convertible terms

[1] G. Lindblom, *The Akamba*, p. 228.
[2] E. S. Hartland, op. cit., I, p. 158.
[3] C. G. and B. Z. Seligman, *Pagan Tribes of the Nilotic Sudan*, p. 109.
[4] C. M. Doke, op. cit., pp. 31-3.

'and ideas; and what in a later stage of Japanese, as
' of Western, civilization is abhorred as incest was in
' Archaic Japanese times the common practice. We also
' hear of marriages with half-sisters, with stepmothers, and
' with aunts; and to wed two or three sisters at the same
' time was a recognized usage '.[1] It is to be noted, however,
that the *Kojiki* and other early writings deal solely with
the doings of gods, kings and chiefs, and there appears to
be no evidence that these practices were followed by
commoners. We may perhaps suppose that in Japan, as
in Uganda and elsewhere, kings practised real, and commoners pretence, brother-sister marriage, for we learn from
the same writer [2] that the latter practice still survives.
When a man has a daughter but no son, he adopts a young
man, who takes his name, and marries his daughter. The
young man is then his wife's legal brother.

P. 172. The husband as brother in the Sudan.

Among the Shiluk, husband and wife address each other
as brother and sister until the first child is born.[3]

P. 196. The god as 'the husband of his mother' in Egyptian theology.

Wiedemann [4] tells us that a great god to whom an
Egyptian temple was dedicated was not regarded as
standing alone. There were companion deities who with
the chief deity formed a triad ' which generally consisted
' of two gods and one goddess; the goddess being the wife
' of the chief god, and the third member of the triad being
' their son. The son was the counterpart of the father, and
' destined to replace him when he should grow old and
' die, according to the law of nature to which even the

---
[1] B. H. Chamberlain, op. cit., p. li.
[2] B. H. Chamberlain, *Things Japanese*, p. 285.
[3] C. G. and B. Z. Seligman, op. cit., p. 55.
[4] A. Wiedemann, *Religion of the Ancient Egyptians*, pp. 103-4.

NOTES

'gods were subject. Thus the son became the father, and
'the Egyptian texts could speak of the gods as eternal;
'for so soon as the elder god vanished he would be suc-
'ceeded by a divine personality precisely similar. In this
'sense also the god was self-begotten, being father to the
'son who was as himself; and he was "the husband of
'"his mother" in that, after the death of his father, he
'had entered upon all rights as regards the goddess of the
'triad, and was in his turn by her the father of the new
'divine son who should one day replace him. This
'scheme of functions provided not only for the unfailing
'continuance of the divinity, but also for the independent
'existence of each of the divine individualities by means
'of which it was carried on. It is complete in all its parts
'except for the goddess; for *a priori*, she would also grow
'old, and pass away, and be superseded. No explanation
'of this omission is given in Egyptian doctrine.'

Since each goddess married two or more gods in succession, it is obvious that the goddesses must have lived much longer than the gods, and I suggest that the doctrine came down from a time when the divine king was killed at the end of a fixed period, and the divine queen married to his successor; that it is in fact the Oedipus myth in another form.

BIBLIOGRAPHY

(Works marked with an asterisk contain discussions of incest origin.)

ACKERMAN, A. S. E. : *Popular Fallacies Explained and Corrected.* London, 1923.
ASTON, W. G. : *Shinto.* London, 1910.
*ATKINSON, J. J., and LANG, A. : *Social Origins and Primal Law.* London, 1903.
*AVEBURY, Lord : *The Origin of Civilization.* London, 1912.
*BRIFFAULT, R. : *The Mothers.* 3 vols. London, 1927.
    Do.   *The Making of Humanity.* London, 1919.
BROWNE, J. C. : *Indian Infanticide, its Origin, Progress and Suppression.* London, 1857.
BUDGE, E. A. WALLIS : *Legends of the Gods.* London, 1912.
CARDINALL, A. W. : *Tales Told in Togoland.* London, 1931.
CHAMBERLAIN, B. H. : *The Kojiki.* Tokyo, 1920.
    Do.   *Things Japanese.* London, 1891.
*CRAWLEY, A. E. : *The Mystic Rose*, 2 vols. London, 1927.
CREW, PROF. A. E., in *An Outline of Modern Knowledge.* London, 1931.
DAWSON, WARREN R. : *The Custom of Couvade.* Manchester, 1929.
    Do.   *Mummification in Australia and America.* JRAI, 1928.

DASENT, SIR G. W. : *The Story of Burnt Njal.* London, 1861.

DOKE, C. M. : *The Lambas of Northern Rhodesia.* London, 1931.

*DORSEY, G. A. : *Civilization.* New York and London, 1931.

DOWSON, J. : *Dictionary of Hindu Mythology.* 5th ed. London, 1913.

DU CHAILLU, P. B. : *The Viking Age.* 2 vols. London, 1889.

*DURKHEIM, E., in *L'Année Sociologique.* Paris, 1898.

ELKIN, A. P. : *The Dieri Kinship System.* JRAI, 1931.
    Do.   *The Social Organization of Australian Tribes,* in *Oceania.* Melbourne, 1931.

*ELLIS, H. HAVELOCK : *Studies in the Psychology of Sex,* 3rd ed., 7 vols. London, 1924.

EMPSON, R. H. W. : *The Cult of the Peacock Angel.* London, 1928.

FARNELL, L. R. : *The Cults of the Greek States.* 5 vols. Oxford, 1921
    Do.   *Greek Hero Cults and Ideas of Immortality.* Oxford, 1921.

FIRTH, RAYMOND : *Primitive Economics of the New Zealand Maori.* London, 1929.
    Do.   *Marriage and the Classificatory System of Relationship.* JRAI, 1930.

FORDE, C. DARYLL : *Ethnography of the Yuma Indians.* Berkeley, Cal., 1931.

FRAZER, SIR J. G. : *The Golden Bough.* 12 vols. London, 1913-18.
    Do.   *The Golden Bough.* Abridged Edition. London, 1923.

BIBLIOGRAPHY

*FRAZER, SIR J. G. *Folklore in the Old Testament.* 3 vols. London, 1918.
* Do. *Totemism and Exogamy.* 4 vols. London, 1910.
Do. *The Fasti of Ovid.* 4 vols. London, 1929.
*FREUD, S. : *Totem and Taboo.* London, 1919.
HARRISON, H. S. : Presidential Address to Section H., British Association, 1929.
HARRISON, JANE : *Themis.* Cambridge, 1912.
HARTLAND, E. S. : *Primitive Paternity.* 2 vols. London, 1909.
HOBHOUSE, L. T. : *Mind in Evolution.* London, 1901.
Do. *Morals in Evolution.* London, 1912.
HOCART, A. M. : *Kingship.* Oxford, 1927.
Do. in *Ceylon Journal of Science*, Section E. 1928.
HOLDSWORTH, W. S. : *History of English Law.* London, 1903.
*HOSE, C., and MCDOUGALL, W. : *The Pagan Tribes of Borneo.* 2 vols. London, 1912.
HOWITT, A. W. : *The Native Tribes of South-East Australia.* London, 1914.
HUGHES, T. P. : *Dictionary of Islam.* London, 1885.
*HUTH, A. H. : *The Marriage of Near Kin.* London, 1875.
JOSEPHUS, FLAVIUS : *Against Apion.*
JUBAINVILLE, ARBOIS DE : *Irish Mythological Cycle.* London, 1884.
KARSTEN, R. : *Studies in South American Anthropology.* Helsingfors, 1920.
KROEBER, A. L. : *Handbook of the Indians of California.* Washington, 1925.

*LINDBLOM, G. : *The Akamba.* Upsala, 1920.
LOWIE, R. H. : *Primitive Society.* London, 1921.
MCDOUGALL, W. : *Social Psychology.* London, 1915.
MAGNUSSON, E., and MORRIS, W. : *The Volsunga Saga.* London, 1870.
*MCLENNAN, J. F. : *Studies in Ancient History.* London, 1886.
*MALINOWSKI, B. : *Sex and Repression in Savage Society.* London, 1927.
MALORY, T. : *Morte Darthur.* Globe ed. London, 1870.
Man, published monthly by the Royal Anthropological Institute.
*MARETT, DR. R. R., in *An Outline of Modern Knowledge.* London, 1931.
MEAD, MARGARET : *Coming of Age in Samoa.* London, 1929.
*MONTAIGNE'S *Essays.* Tr. Florio.
MURRAY, MARGARET A. : *The Witch-Cult in Western Europe.* Oxford, 1921.
*PERRY, W. J. : *The Children of the Sun.* London, 1923.
Do. *The Megalithic Culture of Indonesia.* Manchester, 1918.
PLUTARCH : *Life of Lycurgus.*
RATTRAY, R. S. : *Ashanti.* Oxford, 1923.
Do. *Ashanti Law and Constitution.* Oxford, 1929.
RIDGEWAY, SIR W. : *The Origin of Tragedy.* Cambridge, 1910.
RIVERS, W. H. R. : *The Todas.* London, 1906.
ROSCOE, J. : *The Baganda.* London, 1911.
Do. *The Northern Bantu.* Cambridge, 1915.
*RUTTER O. : *The Pagans of North Borneo.* London, 1929.

*Seligman, B. Z. : *Incest and Descent.* JRAI, 1929.
Seligman, C. G., and B. Z. : *Pagan Tribes of the Nilotic Sudan.* London, 1932.
Skeat, W. W., and Blagden, C. O. : *The Pagan Tribes of the Malay Peninsula.* 2 vols. London, 1906.
*Smith, G. Elliot : *Human History.* London, 1930.
*Smith, W. Robertson : *Kinship and Marriage in Early Arabia.* Cambridge, 1885.
Smyth, R. Brough : *The Aborigines of Victoria.* 2 vols. Melbourne, 1870.
Sophocles : *King Oedipus.* Tr. L. Campbell. London, 1906.
*Spencer, Herbert : *Principles of Sociology.* 2 vols. London, 1872.
Stayt, H. : *The Bavenda.* Oxford, 1831.
Sudan Notes and Records, Vol. 1. Cairo, 1918.
*Sumner and Keller : *The Science of Society.* Newhaven, 1927.
Thirlwall, C. : *History of Greece.* 5 vols. London, 1836.
Thomas, Bertram: *Arabia Felix.* London, 1932.
Do. *Among Some Unknown Tribes of South Arabia.* JRAI, 1929.
Thomson, Sir A. : in *An Outline of Modern Knowledge.* London, 1931.
Torday, E. : *On the Trail of the Bushongo.* London, 1925.
Do. *Dualism in Bantu Religion and Social Organization.* JRAI, 1928.
Tozzer, A. M. : *Social Origins and Social Continuities.* New York, 1925.
Wagner, W., and Macdowall, M. W. : *Asgard and the Gods.* London, 1886.

WALES, H. G. Q. : *Siamese State Ceremonies.* London, 1931.
*WELLS, H. G. : *The Work, Wealth and Happiness of Mankind.* London, 1932.
*WELLS, H. G., and M. D., and HUXLEY, J. : *The Science of Life.* London, 1930.
WESTERMANN, D. : *The Shilluk People.* Berlin, n.d.
*WESTERMARCK, E. : *The History of Human Marriage.* 3 vols. London, 1921.
*   Do.   *The Origin and Development of Moral Ideas.* 2 vols. London, 1908.
WIEDEMANN, A. : *Religion of the Ancient Egyptians.* London, 1897.
WIMBERLEY, L. C. : *Folklore in the English and Scottish Ballads.* Chicago, 1928.
WOOLLEY, C. LEONARD : *The Sumerians.* Oxford, 1928.
YERKES, R. M., and A. W. : *The Great Apes.* Yale, 1929.
ZUCKERMAN, S. : *The Social Life of Apes and Monkeys.* London, 1932.

INDEX

Abel, 146
Adae, 112
Adam, 82, 161-2, 170
Aeneid, 47
Aesop's Fables, 19
Africa, adultery in, 36; aged killed in, 74; cross-cousin marriage in, 104; magic in, 89; menstruation in, 110-12; myths of, 158-60; queen-killing in, 165; ritual combat in, 40-2
Agathias, 81, 85
Ainu, 190
Akamba, flood myth, 157, 198; levirate, 183; marriage rite, 41; menstruation, 112; mother-in-law, 118; visit bride by stealth, 120
Albania, 183
Aleuts, 13
Alfred the Great, 137
Algonkin, 121
Al-Hallâj, 150
Allah, 45
America, cross-cousin marriage in, 104; divorce in, 35; magic in, 89; menstruation in, 110, 115; mummification in, 133-4; myths of, 154-6; old people killed in, 73; temporary marriage in, 37
Amos, 162
Amyraut, 83, 85
Anals, 152
Anaximenes, 167
Animals, 10-12
Anuak, 199
Apache, 116
Apis, 187
Apo, 112
Apollo, 148
Aquinas, Thomas, 82, 86

Arab, marriage, 12, 36, 99, 105-6; myths, 149, 150; paternity, 186; rite, 150, 165
Arapahos, 118
Argentine, 11
Argos, 166
Aristotle, 81, 85
Arizona, 169
Artemis, 148
Arthur, 150
Aryan, 74
Ashanti, cross-cousin marriage, 104; incest, 2-5; law, 53; menstruation, 112; paternity, 181, 183
Asiatic divorce, 35
Assam, 41, 104, 152, 169
Assiniboin, 121
Athens, 59, 148
Atkinson, J. J., 33-7, 49, 71, 84, 86, 98
Australia, absence of houses in, 21; absence of jealousy in, 36; cross-cousin marriage in, 104; dual organization in, 124; ignorance of paternity in, 15; incest in, 6, 15, 80, 106; law in, 61-2; magic in, 89; menstruation in, 110, 112; mother-in-law in, 116-17; mummification in, 133-4; myths of, 157; rabbits in, 10
Avebury, Lord, 39, 85
Awemba, 105
Azande, 159
'Azîz bin Khâlu, 150

Babylonia, 89, 146, 151
Bacon, Francis, 90
Baganda. See Uganda
Baila, 111
Balearic Is., 185
Balkans, 100

Banks Is., 104
Bantu, 127, 167
Banyoro, 42, 160
Bashilele, 158
Basoga, 159–60
Bavenda, 172
Bechuana, 104
Beduins, 12
Bel, 146, 151
Bellerophon, 193
Bengal, 110, 120
Beni Hilal, 149
Bergelmir, 148
Beza, Theodore, 82, 85
Bhils, 151
Blood-money, 45
Boat burial, 154, 159, 198
Bogota, 160
Bohemia, 112
Bolivia, 156
Borneo, boat burial in, 159; couvade in, 190; creation legend in, 145; ignorance of paternity in, 15; incest in, 3, 174; myths of, 150–3; wives visited by stealth in, 121
Bororos, 121
Brahmans, 104
Brazil, 104, 110, 121
Bride-price, 35, 41–5, 52
Briffault, Mr. R., on dual organization, 106; on inbreeding, 10–13; on incest origin, 49, 50, 86, 98; on marriage, 184; on marriage by capture, 42, 43, 45; on marriage in Egypt, 80; on menstruation, 114; on mothers-in-law, 119; on wives visited by stealth, 121
Buddha, 127, 151
Burma, 41, 43, 104, 106, 120, 134
Burning of heretics, 27
Burton, Robert, 82, 85
Burton, Sir Richard, 12
Bushmen, 40, 123
Bushongo, 158
Bu Zeid, 149–150

Cain, 146
California, 101, 127, 141, 176, 190

Calymnos, 112
Cambodia, 124
Cambridgeshire, 90
Canary Is., 133
Canon law, 83
Caribs, 104, 118, 121, 190
Carthagena, 84
Caucasus, 120
Celebes, 13, 152, 174
Central Asia, adultery in, 37
Central Europe, 12
Ceram, 111
Ceylon, 104, 124
Chambers, 99
Charlemagne, 35
Cher, 9
Cherokees, 118
China, avoidance in, 117; marriage laws of, 101, 104, 108, 185; myths of, 154
Chiriguanos, 156
Chittagong, 41, 145
Chota Nagpur, 145
Christian marriage laws, 26, 100, 101, 107, 172
Christmas, 44
Chrysippus, 81
Circumcision, 54
Clothru, 149
Commemoration, 43–5
Colorado, 143, 156
Congo, 36, 122
'Construction, instinct of', 21
Cook, Captain, 10
Corinth, 1, 195
Couvade, 189–90
Crawley, A. E., 42, 80, 86, 98
Cree Indians, 36
Creon, 195
Crew, Prof. F. A. E., 13
Crimthann, 149
Cronus, 147
Cross-cousin marriage, 12, 102–4
Cuchulain, 15
Cyrenaica, 185

Dancing, 95
Dane law, 58
Dawson, Mr. Warren R., 112, 133–4, 190 n.

INDEX

Dayaks, 152, 174
Dead, disposal of, 55
Deaf-mutism, 9, 13
Delawares, 110
Delphi, 1
Déné Indians, 111
Deucalion, 148
Dictionaries, 99
Diodorus, 185
Dieri, 105, 180
Dionysus, 148
Dog licences, 46
Dorsey, G. A., 98
Doughty, C. M., 12
Dual organization, 60, 78, 106, 124
Du Chaillu, P. B., 56
Dugard, 83
Durkheim, Prof. E., on dual organization, 106; on incest origin, 77–8, 86; on menstruation, 114; on myth, 138
Dusuns, 145, 153

Easter I., 36
East Indies, 104, 110, 111, 190
Egypt, creation rite in, 166; magic in, 89; marriage of near kin in, 8, 80, 168–9, 171, 194; mummification in, 133–5, 187; myths of, 146–7, 150, 200; sacrifice in, 165
Eleusinian mysteries, 142
Ellis, Dr. Havelock, on instinct, 21; on incest origin, 29–32, 85, 98; on menstruation, 113
Endogamy, defined 12; effects of, 13, 76
England, laws of, 57–8, 182; matrilocal marriage in, 40; menstruation in, 112
Eskimo, 36, 80
Euhemerism, 137, 158, 167
Euphrates, 151
Europe, beliefs about inbreeding in, 14; bridal custom in, 41
Exodus, 58
Exogamy, 5, 12, 26, 61, 102
Eyes, sun and moon made from, 142, 146, 147, 164, 193, 198

Farnell, Dr. L. R., 192
Fiji, cousin-marriage in, 12, 104; creation rite in, 141; moieties divided by water, 127; wives visited by stealth, 121
Firth, Prof. R., 52 n., 76, 86
Flamen Dialis, 173
Forde, Prof. C. Daryll, 142
Forèatines, 9
Formosa, 41, 153
France, cousin-marriage in, 3, 83; inbreeding in, 9; marriage customs in, 185
Frazer, Sir James, on dual organization, 106, 124; on early kingship, 168, 194; on incest origin, 59–63, 76, 86, 98; on magic, 88–91, 97; on myth, 137; on parricide, 73; on the Pentateuch, 48, 58; on sacrifice, 174
Freud, Dr. S., 70–4, 86, 93, 98
Frey and Freya, 149
Fu-Hi, 154
Function, 26, 27, 49, 97
Furies, 45

Galelarese, 13
Garos, 41
Genesis, 146, 161, 170
Germans, 12
Germany, 90
Gilbert Is., 111, 142
Gillen, F. J., 61
Glenfinlass, 9
Gloucestershire, 41
Gorillas, 33, 34
Greece, horror of incest in, 3; human sacrifice in, 165; kingship in, 194; laws of, 59; magic in, 89; marriage in, 101, 106, 189; myths of, 147–8; philosophers of, 59, 96, 167
Grimm, J., 74
Guiana, 104

Haida Indians, 155
Hamlet, 140
Hammurabi, 53–4
Hanafis, 101

Hareskin Indians, 154
Harold, King, 44
Harrison, Dr. H. S., 132–3
Harrison, Jane, 138
Harûn ar-Rashîd, 35
Harvey, Wm., 184
Hasluck, Mrs., 183
Hastings, 44
Hawaii, 160
Helsingfors, 42
Hera, 147, 166, 189
Heracles, 193
Herero, 116
Herodotus, 185
Hierapolis, 151
Hindu, avoidance, 117; marriage, 103, 108; menstruation, 111; mummification, 134; myths, 141, 142, 151; paternity, 186
Hobhouse, Prof. L. T., 22, 24–8, 85, 97
Hocart, Mr. A. M., on couvade, 190 n.; on dual organization, 124, 127; on marriage, 38, 80; on myth, 138, 141–2, 144, 161 n.
Horace, 156
Hose, Dr. C., 34
Howitt, A. W., 127
Human sacrifice, 52, 165, 175
Huth, A. H., on inbreeding, 8–10, 13; on incest origin, 81–4, 85, 98
Huxley, Prof. J., 88

Iceland, 56–7, 199
Igorot, 152
India, adultery in, 37; couvade in, 190; dual organization in, 124; magic in, 89; marriage in, 4, 5, 104–5, 185; mummification in, 133; myths of, 151; sacrifice in, 165, 175
Indus, 124
Inhibitions, 30–1
Ireland, 41, 149, 185
Iroquois, 121
Isis, 147
Islam, 100
Italy, 37, 115
Izanagi, 154, 197–8

Japan, 120, 154, 190, 197–200
Jason, 193
Java, 9, 104
Jews, conservatism of, 59; levirate among, 183; marriage of, 101, 107, 165
Jocasta, 1, 2, 195
Johnson, Dr., 99
Johnston, Sir H., 36
Joseph, 15
Josephus, 59

Kamars, 151
Kamchadals, 41
Kariera, 105
Karok, 141
Karsten, Dr. R., 42
Kayans, 159
Keb, 146
Khartum, 158
Khasis, 120
Khepera, 146
Khnoumou, 146
Kikuyu, 174
Kingship, divine, 79
Kojiki, 197, 199, 200
Kôli, 127
Kombees, 127
Kootenay, 155
Krachi, 197
Kukumat, 143
Kumis, 145
Kurdistan, 74
Kurils, 120
Kutree, 127

Laius, 1
Lambas, 197–9
Lang, Andrew, 76
Lau Is., 127
Lawman, 56
Lawrence, 84
Leviticus, 9
Lif and Lifthrasir, 149
Lindblom, Dr. G., 167
Lisus, 43
Lithuania, 148
Locke, John, 26
Lord Mayor, 139, 140
Lot, 161

INDEX

Loucheux, 155
Lowie, Prof. R. H., 28, 85
Lugaid, 149
Luther, Martin, 82, 85, 173
Lutyens, Sir Edwin, 21
Lycurgus, 59

McCardie, Mr. Justice, 30 n.
Macareus, 32, 195–6
McDougall, Prof. W., 21, 34, 97
Macedonia, 41
McLennan, J. F., 39, 85
Madagascar, 174
Madras, 111
Majaji, 158
Malasi, 178
Malaya, 89, 122, 153
Malinowski, Prof. B., on incest origin, 18–20, 66–8, 86, 98, 178; on taboo, 93; on virginity among savages, 49
Mandans, 155
Manipur, 120
Manu, 151
Marett, Dr. R. R., on incest origin, 64–8, 86; on myth, 136; on symbolism, 114
Marindineeze, 143
Masai, 175
Maspero, Sir Gaston, 169
Matrilocal marriage, 40, 103
Medes, 52
Mediterranean, 173
Melanesia, 89, 104, 106, 133
Mercian law, 58
Mesopotamia, 150
Mexican, 145, 156, 165
Michoacans, 145
Mindanao, 13
Moala, 127
Modoc Indians, 117
Mohave, 176
Moluccas, 190
Mongols, 37
Montaigne, 32, 96
Montesquieu, 84, 85
Moorish proverb, 15
Moravia, 112
Mordred, 150
Morgan, L. H., 15, 85

Morocco, 15, 41
Mosaic law, 9, 48, 110
Moses, 47, 193
Moslem, 45, 56, 100, 105, 106, 107, 172, 185
Mothers, human, 24
Mufti, 56
Mummification, 132–5, 188
Mundas, 145, 151
Murray river, 112
Muruts, 153
Myhee river, 127

Na Arean, 142
Nablus, 185
Nagas, 120
Napier, 61
Nasamones, 185
Navahoes, 118
Nayar, 111
Nevada, 118
New Britain, 116
New Caledonia, 15, 104
New Guinea, 15, 16, 104, 110, 116, 121, 143
New Hebrides, 37, 104
New Ireland, 104
New Mexico, 155
New Zealand, 10, 157
Nigeria, 105
Nile, 124, 154, 158
Niu-kua, 154
Njal, Burnt, 56
Njord, 148
Noah, 161
Nordic, 56, 142, 173
Norse, 148–50
Norway, 56
Novatian, 81, 85
Nut, 146
Nyakang, 158–9
Nyimi Lele, 158

Oedipus, 1, 2, 32, 192–6, 201
Oedipus complex, 74
Ordeal, trial by, 54
Orinoco, 110
Ortho-cousin marriage, 12, 105
Orthodox, 172
Osiris, 147, 188

Pacific Is., 110, 124, 185
Palestine, 189
Palestinian boar, 48
Pangwe, 117
Parricide, 1, 71-4
Parsees, 55
Partholon, 149
Paternity, ignorance of, 14, 15, 184, 197
Pelew Is., 156
Penance, 73
Pentateuch, 47
Perry, Dr. W. J., 69, 152, 167 n.
Perseus, 193
Persia, 8, 37, 80, 111, 120, 194
Peru, 160
Peter Pan, 192-3
Pharaoh, 141, 147
Philippines, 152
Philo, 81, 85
Pima Indians, 156
Pitcairn Is., 9
Pitt-Rivers, Gen., 131
Plains Indians, 153
Plato, 32, 81, 85
Pliny, 15, 89
Plutarch, 81, 120
Polonius, 140
Polynesia, 74, 104
Pope Gregory I, 82, 83, 85
Popes, 100, 173, 176
'Primal law', 33-5
Procopius, 74
Progress idea of, 20
Prometheus, 148
Psycho-analysis, 70-2, 119, 136
Pueblo Indians, 121, 169
Punjab, 111
Purgatory, 73
Purusha, 142
Pygmies, 36, 122
Pyrrha, 148

Queen-killing, 165
Quetelet, 21

Ra, 147
Rachel, 15
Radcliffe-Brown, Prof. A., 45 n.
Ragnarok, 149

Raguel, 171
Rameses II, 188
Rattray, Captain, R. S., 2, 4, 112
Reflex action, 22
Remorse, 71-3
Rhea, 147
Rhodesia, 105, 111
Ridgeway, Sir W., 137
Ritual, 43-5
Rivers, Dr. W. H. R., 124
Rohâna river, 127
Romans, 89, 98, 111, 173, 181, 187
Romulus, 193
Russian rite, 178

Sabbath, 48
St. Augustine, 15, 81, 85
St. Chrysostom, 81, 85
Sâkya, 127
Samaritans, 185
Samoa, 161, 173
Samoyeds, 120
Santals, 151
Scotland, 37, 41, 89
Seligman, B. Z. (Mrs. C. G.), 65-8, 86, 98
Sellenger's Round, 48
Semele, 148
Seth, 146
Settegast, Prof., 12
Sexual selection, 30
Shafais, 101
Shiahs, 100
Shiluk, 154, 158-9, 200
Shu, 146
Siam, 124, 154
Siberia, 73, 104, 110, 120
Sigmund, 150
Signy, 150
Sinfjotli, 150
Sister, advances made by, 145, 146, 147, 149, 150, 151, 152, 153, 157, 165, 198
Skeat, 99
Smell, sense of, 23
Smith, Prof. G. Elliott, 79, 86, 98, 132, 133
Smith, Dr. W. Robertson, 16
Socrates, 81, 85
Solomon Is., 16, 76

INDEX

Solomon, Song of, 151
'Sortes Virgilianae', 47
Sparta, 59, 120
Spencer, Herbert, 39, 85
Spencer, Sir B., 61
Sphinx, 1, 192, 196
Statius, 81, 85
Stuarts, 9
Suffolk, 90
Sudan, 190
Sumatra, 104
Sunnis, 100

Tahiti, 156
Tano river, 112
Taylor, Bp. Jeremy, 83, 86
Tefnunt, 146
Tengger Hills, 9
Teutons, 74
Thales, 167
Thebes, 1, 195
Theseus, 193
Thesmophoria, 148
Thing, Norse, 56
Thomas, Mr. Bertram, 149 n., 150
Thomson, Sir A., 13
Thor, 149
Thorgeir, 56-7
Thurii, 59
Thyestes, 32, 196
Tiamat, 151
Tibet, 104
Tierra del Fuego, 21
Tigris, 150
Tikopia, 76
Timor, 104
Tipperah, 120
Titans, 148
Tobias, 171
Tobit, 171
Todas, 37, 181-2
Tonga, 161
Toradja, 152
Torday, E., 127
Torres Straits, 131
Totem, 71, 73, 77
Tozzer, Prof. A. M., 94 n.
Transjordan, 185
Transvaal, 158

Trobriand Is., 15, 157, 177-8, 197
Tucapacha, 145
Tumbou, 127
Tylor, Sir E. B., 15, 85, 131

Uganda, avoidance in, 178; marriage in, 104, 159, 172, 189, 200; mother-in-law in, 119; myth of, 146; royal houses in, 127; twins in, 160
Uranus, 147

Vaccination, 47
Victoria, tribes of, 127, 157
Virgil, 15
Volsunga Saga, 150

Wagogo, 118
Wahehe, 118, 174
Wales, 41
Webster, 99
Wells, Mr. H. G., 39, 85, 88
Wends, 74
Westermarck, Dr. E., on incest, 4; on incest origin, 15, 16, 24, 85; on marriage, 38; on marriage by capture, 42; on mother-in-law, 119
West Indies, 185, 190
West Saxon law, 58
William the Conqueror, 137, 188
Winamwanga, 105
Wood-pigeons, 22
Woolley, Mr. C. L., 53
Woto, 158

Yakuts, 120
Yama, 151
Yerkes, Mr. R. M., 20
Yezidis, 150
Ymir, 142, 148
Yucatan, 116
Yuma, 142-3

Zeno, 81
Zeus, 147, 189
Zoroaster, 15
Zuckerman, Mr. S., 20
Zunis, 155